White Water

RUNNING THE WILD RIVERS
OF NORTH AMERICA

RUNNING
OF

A WALKER GALLERY BOOK

WALKER AND COMPANY

720 FIFTH AVENUE, NEW YORK, N.Y. 10019

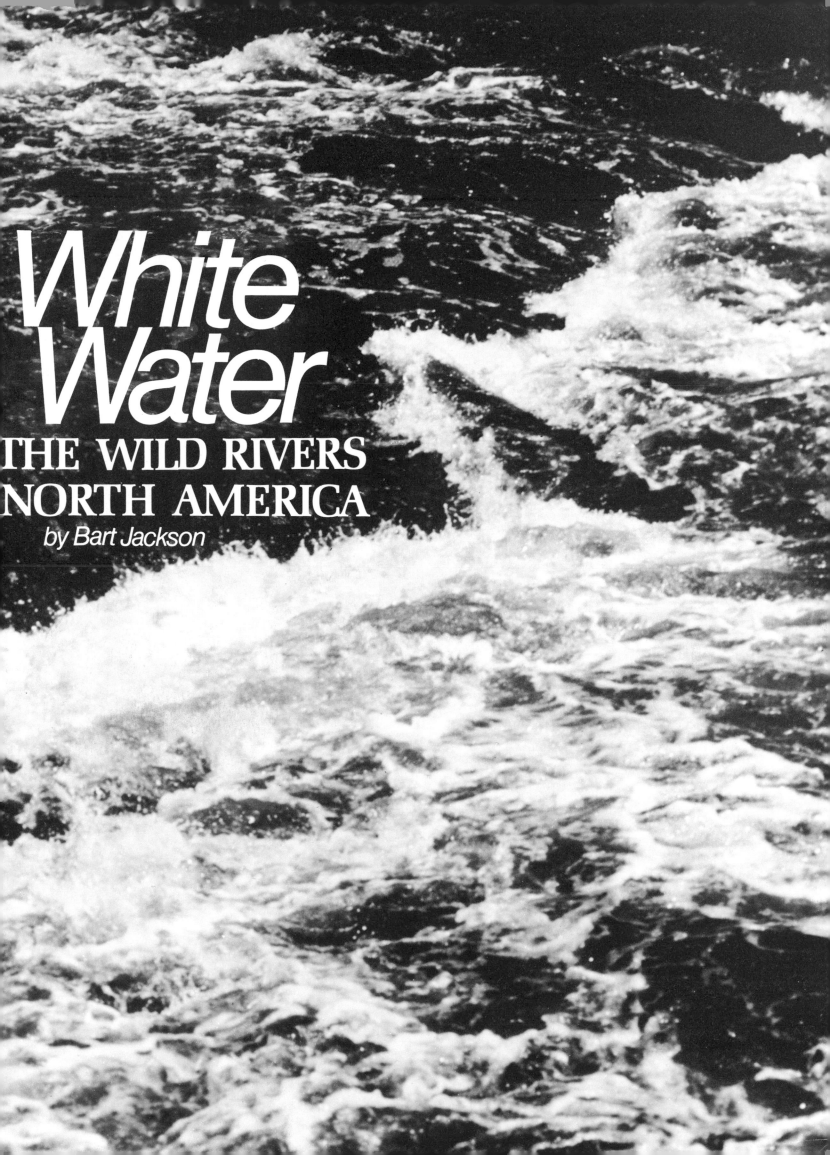

White Water

THE WILD RIVERS NORTH AMERICA

by Bart Jackson

STAFF

EDITOR: David Kellogg
ART DIRECTOR: Barbara Huntley
MANAGING EDITOR: Andrea Curley
RESEARCH: Jean Miller

First published in the United States of America in 1979 by the Walker Publishing Company, Inc.

Published simultaneously in Canada by Beaverbooks, Limited, Pickering, Ontario

Cloth   ISBN: 0-8027-0598-7
Paper   ISBN: 0-8027-7132-7

Library of Congress Catalog Card Number: 77-93731

Printed in Japan by Dai Nippon Printing Co., Ltd., Tokyo

10 9 8 7 6 5 4 3 2 1

Contents

Introduction

It is said that if there is magic in the earth, it flows in water. To stand on a bank and stare into a rapid releases the spirit. But to join with the water, blend its energies with yours, and move as part of it instills an unparalleled exhilaration and awe. It is the aim of this book to reveal a little of that magic, guide you to where it lies, and give a glimpse of that special excitement felt by men and women devoted to running rivers.

Rushing water is the most powerful, incessant force nature allows us to witness. It is everywhere and, like all of nature, beautiful in its diversity. Rivers vary not only from one to another, but within their own length. Each has its own character, yet flows in universal patterns. And each stream demands something unique of a boater's skills. The rivers described here are selected to span the broad spectrum of white water and its challenges.

Once whitewater paddling has enthralled you, you will never again look at a stream in the same way. Every eroded gulley and backyard brook comes under scrutiny as a possible stretch of white water. Eyes search a foot-wide trickle for a channel, and muscles flex, calculating the strokes it will take to dodge this root and that pebble. In the end you sacrifice some ignorant wonder, but you gain an almost reverent appreciation of water. Said one paddler, "Niagara Falls was pretty impressive, but those rapids above it *really* scared the heck out of me."

The avid "river rat" also becomes enmeshed in a community ripe with ritual, myth, and legend. Every river has a reputation and each rapid a name. The perils of "Broken Paddle" and "Banzai" are buzzed abroad with no less marvel than that of ancient Greeks telling of Scylla and Charybdis. This common understanding and experience draws paddlers together and makes them live for boating weekends.

Within the river descriptions, I have tried to relay some of these local legends (most grounded at least slightly in fact) along with some of the common paddlers' rituals. They are as inherent a part of white water as paddling technique and numb fingers.

Getting Started: Today, whitewater paddling stands among the legion of newly rediscovered sports that make up America's great rush back to the outdoors. Unfortunately, most people still view white water through an unrealistic kaleidoscope of liquor ads, movies, and fading Boy Scout memories.

Your best bet is to avoid the romanticism and enter white water with a greediness for instruction. Enthusiasm, more than skill, determines a neophyte's acceptance, and the eager learner will find more friendly advice than he could ever use.

The ideal first step is to search out a club and get into its instruction program. (See club list on p. 124.) Experiment and decide what kind of boating you want to do: canoe or kayak, competition or cruising. Only after you've made these choices should you buy any equipment—and only with the help of local experts.

Whatever kind of paddling you choose, work up *gradually* to the level of water you can handle, not just survive. To advance your skill demands effort, experience, and solid coaching. Whitewater boating, while no longer new, retains an atmosphere of informality, with most methods and techniques being passed from mentor to neophyte. Books and instruction weekends help, but your greatest development will come from that special expert and willing teacher who takes you under his wing. Beg for his criticism.

Finally, getting started is not easy. Much of whitewater paddling is cold, wet, miserable, and darn hard work. The beginner must endure all this, along with his own fears, frustrations, and nearly total exhaustion. But as confidence, skill, and muscle tone start to build and you begin to work your way through seeming disasters, the pain will fade and you can savor a taste of the magic.

How To Use This Book

This volume presents a trip-planning guide to 72 whitewater streams throughout America. For the beginner, or even the hopeful, it offers a place to start: some easy, forgiving stretches of river nearby that can be run with a minimum of risk. For the experienced boater, it provides more challenging water, plus a vista into regions beyond his own. Most New Englanders, for example, remain totally unaware of the different styles of white water available in Minnesota, The Ozarks, Washington— or these areas' potential for extended trips in all seasons.

I have divided the continental United States into eight regions, each distinctive, but widely varied within itself. These regions are generally based on tradition, traveling range, and, to some extent, geography. The listing of streams within each region is by no means exhaustive. They were selected to give an overview, representing degrees of river characteristics, difficulty, and popularity. (If you want more within your region, most areas have thorough local guides. See bibliography p. 126.) To find individual rivers, check the index.

To plan a day or weekend trip in your area, turn to your region's chapter and examine the map and generalized regional description. Then thumb through the area rivers and scan the tabular material preceding the text. Check the river *Classification* and capsule *Description* to make sure this stream lies within your ability range and paddling style. Then check the *Running Season* so you don't end up carting your boat down a dry river bed. Most streams flood with the spring snowmelt and drop steadily through a dry summer season, then rise to varying degrees with the fall rains. But river levels change from year to year and the *Running Season* can only be a general reference. Local boaters and gauge readers can give more up-to-date information.

The *Location* tells the approximate driving time from the nearest major paddling city in the state. The *Standard Runs* are designed for day or weekend trips. Each section of river from the put-in (where you start) to the take-out (where you finish) lists mileage that can be paddled in one day unless otherwise stated. The put-in and take-out towns are all listed on state road maps; additional directions are given to the river bank where necessary.

Once you find a river that seems both inviting and possible, read the text. This is not a rock-by-rock whitewater guide. It does not map the river by hundred-yard sections. Rather, it describes what you will experience on the river and what to expect from it. It also covers what kinds of paddling are done on this stream, gives an overview of the challenge and hazards, and describes specifically some of the larger rapids on the run. It is what you would learn by talking with a local expert who has paddled this section of the river for years.

Each stream is classified according to difficulty using the American Canoe Association's rating system of 1 through 6. (See box at end of glossary for description.) But it must be understood that any river classification is only approximate. No river is static. A Class-2 creek can flood overnight and become a Class 4. A Class 1 + can be a Class 5 just a few miles upstream. In addition, boaters seldom agree on which rivers are Class 2 and which are 3. I hope I have erred on the side of safety, but, in the end, the final precautions must lie with the individual paddler. It is his job to check local clubs, gauges, and authorities, and to place common sense above bravado.

Finally, rivers change, and books go out of date. It is possible that there are some errors in these river descriptions. If you note any, instead of just telling your paddling buddy, please tell me: Bart Jackson, c/o Walker and Co., 720 Fifth Avenue, N.Y.C. 10019.

—B.J.

Glossary

boulder garden A rock garden *(see below)* on a larger scale.

bow The front of a boat.

C-1 Originally a racing classification for any one-person canoe. Term now covers all types of decked racing boats. Similar to a kayak in appearance, the C-1 is virtually watertight. Small cockpit is covered by sprayskirt.

C-2 Two-man canoe; usually decked to prevent swamping.

canoe Flatwater or whitewater craft. Can be open or decked; paddler kneels or sits and uses a single-bladed paddle. Minimum width is 70 cm., length ranges from 13 to 17 feet.

carry A short portage. Hauling yourself and canoe around an impassable section of river.

cascade Very steep, but not quite vertical drop into a pool.

chute A break in a ledge or dam which permits running it without doing a nosedive.

decked boat Usually a K-1, C-1, or C-2; a narrow boat, closed except for small cockpit. A tight-fitting sprayskirt attaches to the cockpit rim and around the paddler's waist. The boat is small, maneuverable, easy to roll upright, and impossible to swamp.

draw A maneuvering stroke used to pull the boat to the on-paddle side.

drop Any steep gradient in the river—either sheer or sloping. The water speeds up and develops rapids.

eddy The still, quiet section of water immediately downstream of an obstruction blocking the main current, and forcing the water to swirl around it. **side eddy:** an eddy formed by an indentation or sharp bend in the river bank. **upstream eddy:** an eddy which runs counter to the current.

ender A hotdogger's stunt: ramming the bow or stern of a closed boat into a vertical wall of water which slams the deck under water and literally stands the boat on end. **pop-up:** Partial ender. Boat lifts up and out of the water in the same manner, but doesn't stand on end.

Eskimo roll A method of using hips and paddle to right yourself after dumping in a watertight kayak or C-1.

hair Big, heavy volume water full of keeper holes and high haystacks; very difficult rapids.

haystacks A series of evenly spaced waves formed by the sheer speed and power of the current. These generally give a harmless, bouncy ride, though high haystacks can swamp open boats.

hotdogger A gung-ho paddler willing to play in all kinds of holes and take all kinds of risks. A state of mind.

hydraulic *(also hole, curler, roller)* A depression in the water at the base of a ledge, dam, or steep drop. Caused by water flowing over an obstacle, dropping, and curling back on itself to form a rolling, stationary wave.

kayak (K-1) A small, maneuverable one-man whitewater craft of Eskimo origin. Paddler sits with legs outstretched and uses a double-bladed paddle. The boat is narrow, approximately 60 cm., with an oval cockpit covered by a sprayskirt.

keeper hole A hole large and powerful enough to hold both boat and paddler and keep them constantly rotating in a mass of foam.

ledge A sheer vertical drop formed by a rock shelf.

open boat A traditional canoe design. Though it cannot be rolled, it can hold large amounts of gear for camping. It can also be sailed.

play To make maneuvers not ordinarily needed for river running, i.e. surfing, pop-ups, enders, eddy turns, sitting in a hole. Playing, in addition to allowing you to show off, sharpens boat control and reduces your fear of water.

pool A still, quiet section of water in center-current immediately below a rapid.

pry A maneuvering stroke which turns the boat to the off-paddle side.

rock garden A section of river littered with any size rocks, leaving only narrow ribbons of water for the boater to follow.

scout To judge *(usually from shore)* whether a particular stretch of water can be run, and to pick the safest route ahead of time.

shoal A shallow stretch of water flowing over gravel and small rocks. Tricky technical work for the paddler—and much boat scraping.

slalom A timed competition designed to test boat maneuvering and speed. For a short section of white water the boater negotiates numbered gates.

sleighride An open stretch of heavy water with bouncy haystacks and few obstacles, that can be run without fear of hitting anything.

staircase A series of ledges which are close together. Paddler must drop from one to another,

zig-zagging back and forth to line up the boat with the right chute.

stern The back of a boat.

surfing Usually, placing bow or stern on the upstream rolling wave at the base of a hole. The paddler can sit motionless on the wave while the current sweeps downstream around him.

technical paddling Weaving through rock gardens and other obstacles; this requires continuous drawing and prying.

undercut Eroded section of rock or river bank which the current has cut away at the base, leaving an overhang of rock or soil at water level. Usually found on the outside of a sharp curve. A real hazard: A boat can be swept under the overhang and the paddler smashed or pinned underwater.

water reading Studying the current and noting signs which indicate possible routes and obstructions.

wildwater race *(Also downriver race.)* A straight, timed race. Boater races a whitewater course, usually 5 to 8 miles long. No artificial maneuvering. Special boats are used which are fast but difficult to turn.

AMERICAN CANOE ASSOCIATION'S
STANDARD RIVER CLASSIFICATION

Class 1. Moving water with a few riffles and small waves. Few or no obstructions.

Class 2. Small scale rapids: waves up to 3 feet, wide clear channels that are obvious without scouting. Some maneuvering required.

Class 3. Rapids with high, irregular waves, often capable of swamping open canoes. Narrow passages often requiring complex maneuvering. May require scouting from shore.

Class 4. Long, difficult rapids with constricted passages often requiring precise maneuvering in very turbulent water. Scouting from shore often necessary. Conditions make rescue difficult.

Decked boaters should be able to Eskimo roll. Generally the upper limit for even expert open boaters.

Class 5. Extremely long, difficult, very violent rapids with highly congested routes. Nearly always must be scouted from shore. Rescue conditions are difficult, and a mishap means considerable hazard to life. Ability to Eskimo roll is essential.

Class 6. Difficulties of Class 5 carried to extreme. Nearly impossible and very dangerous. For teams of experts only, at favorable water levels and with all precautions.

NORTHEAST

Rocks. Connecticut farmers curse them, hikers scramble over them, and whitewater enthusiasts smash boats against them. Northeasterners boast the rockiest, coldest rivers in the country and, perhaps less accurately, the fastest rock-dodging reflexes. Running off either side of the Appalachians, which form a rocky spine along the eastern seaboard, are vast networks of boulder-choked, technically tricky streams.

Admitting that generalizations are just that, Northeastern rivers are typically narrow, winding, and short. Streams with more than fifteen miles of white water are the exception, and a continuous rapid of more than half a mile is considered rare. Rapids are usually formed by a powerful current washing over a labyrinth of small-to-mid-size boulders or a vertical ledge. These obstacles check the water speed of even the steepest rivers.

But if the rivers are a little slower and the volume a little lower (six-foot haystacks are considered very big in this region), the technical challenge is second to none. The next rock is always inches away. And the legendary solution—"Just close your eyes and paddle like hell!"—means sure destruction in the Northeast.

New England paddlers hit the rivers when the ice breaks in early March. The runoff normally crests in April and turns to a trickle in mid- or late June. Summer runs are sparse, but in some areas autumn rains frequently raise rivers to temporarily boatable levels. Throughout the spring, rivers are dangerously cold (34°–40°), and a paddler without a wet suit or waterproofed change of clothes is just begging for hypothermia.

Tradition plays a strong part in Northeastern boating. While many boaters live solely to tear up the slalom course in a fiberglass K-1, there exist a large number who still head for the campsite in a canvas canoe with a hand-carved ash paddle.

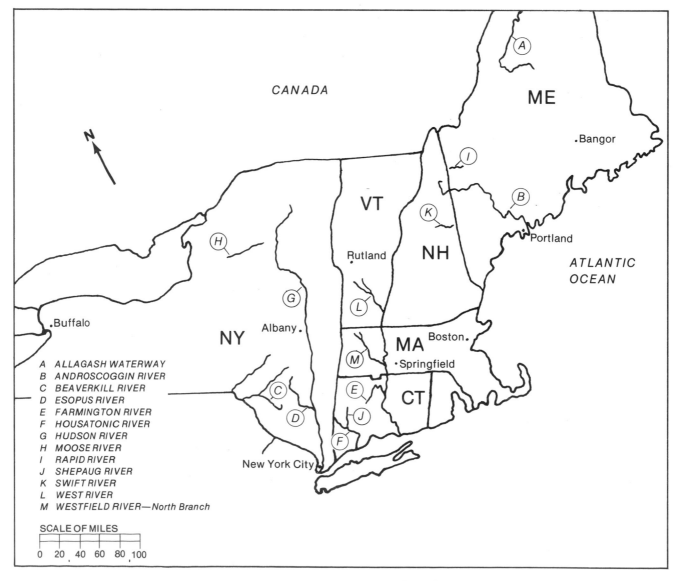

CANADA

ME

.Bangor

VT

Rutland
.

NH

Portland
.

ATLANTIC
OCEAN

.Buffalo

NY

Albany .

Boston .

MA

.Springfield

CT

New York City .

A   ALLAGASH WATERWAY
B   ANDROSCOGGIN RIVER
C   BEAVERKILL RIVER
D   ESOPUS RIVER
E   FARMINGTON RIVER
F   HOUSATONIC RIVER
G   HUDSON RIVER
H   MOOSE RIVER
I   RAPID RIVER
J   SHEPAUG RIVER
K   SWIFT RIVER
L   WEST RIVER
M   WESTFIELD RIVER—North Branch

SCALE OF MILES

0   20   40   60   80   100

NEW ENGLAND
Pine and ice (opposite) are inherent parts of paddling.
And icebreaking may begin as early as February.

Rapid River

CLASS: 4

DESCRIPTION: Narrow, occasionally broadening to a pond; heavy water; ledges and large scattered boulders.

STANDARD RUN: Put in below Middle Dam below Richardson Lake; 6 mi. to Cedar Stump; 2 more mi. to take-out across Lake Umbagog.

LOCATION: On Me./N.H. border, 4½ hrs. N of Boston; above White Mountain Natl. Forest.

RUNNING SEASON: End of June to mid-October; be sure to call Bill Grove (207) 784-4501 for water release info.

On a topographical map the Rapid looks like just another calm little stream meandering quietly between two lakes, here and there broadening into a pond—just another flat section of the Rangely Lake chain. Don't believe it! For six short miles, this narrow heavy-water stream plunges from pond to pond on a trail that hits the paddler with every kind of whitewater surprise imaginable. It is a New England expert's paradise.

The rapids are varied and tricky with seven-foot haystacks that make it for closed boats only. For the first mile or so below the Middle Dam put-in, you are lulled into security by some bouncy Class-3 standing waves in an easy boulder field. You stop in Pond-on-the-River, take a swim, carry around Lower Dam, and tell yourself all is well. Then, for the next four miles, holes leap out from everywhere. The river twists around the blind corners of S-Turn, where foamy pillows hide ominous rocks underneath. But despite its furtive nastiness, the Rapid is an exquisite river for playing. Pools with swift rips, the long curler at Smooth Ledge, and vest-pocket eddies make it a river to work your way down slowly.

This is not a stream for the roadside river runner who wants to dart out of his apartment, surf a hydraulic for a few hours, and come home. Isolated by the Rangely Lakes, the best way to reach the Rapid is to put in at South Arm, Maine, and paddle four miles across Richardson Lake to Middle Dam. Less energetic paddlers may put in at Erroll, New Hampshire, and have Mr. Skip Rowe at Lakewood Camps shuttle them twelve miles across Lake Umbagog behind a motorboat.

Since you cannot easily make a weekend trip of the Rapid, take a week off and camp. The nearby Appalachian Trail, the remote beauty of the Rangely Lakes, plus a river you can train on all day in a forest of maple, pine, and sparkling white birch all make for an area that demands enough time to appreciate fully.

Swift River

CLASS: 4–5

DESCRIPTION: Big, powerful, very rocky; high drops, large standing waves; tight and fast.

STANDARD RUN: Put in at Rocky Gorge (scenic rest area on Kancamagus Hwy.—Rte. 100); 6 to 7 mi. along the Hwy.

LOCATION: 70 mi. N of Manchester, N.H., in White Mountain Natl. Park; 50 mi. W of Portland, Me.

RUNNING SEASON: Late March to June.

No one will ever put a slalom course on the Swift: The last glacier took care of that. Take the power and speed of a Class-5 sleigh ride and pump it over a six-mile jumble of bulldozer-size rocks and you have the Swift—one of the toughest, most technical rivers in New England.

Legendary as a boat destroyer, this is not the run for a brand new, three-layer, 17-pound racing K-1. Nor is it the place for any type of open boat. The standard run starts below a fifteen-foot falls with some Class-3 warm-up ledges that too quickly become Class 4. Lower Falls is a standard carry for all but the experts, where the current squeezes between two boulders and becomes a two-stage, ten-foot waterfall with rocks at the bottom of each stair. There is little letup. The current sweeps the boater along narrow tongues of jetting white water that cover the ledges and broad table rocks. While the river is medium width, the tongue that the paddler is on is seldom wider than a slalom gate.

The Gorge, The Staircase, and others in the last half of the run form a continuous labyrinth that demands the quickest reaction time and best water-reading ability of any paddler. The Swift is dangerous. If you do not feel up to it, run the Saco, Androscoggin, or take a hike in the White Mountains. Do not offer yourself up as a sacrifice to the people-eating holes of this river.

If you have never seen top-end white water running, you can follow the entire run along the Kancamagus Highway. And if you are looking for a whitewater instructor, just wait by the take-out and choose any paddler who has survived the Swift at high water.

SWIFT RIVER
Sweeping over a drop and punching through a curler. (above) Note how the sternman leans back to lighten the bow and allow it to rise. Paddling solo (below) requires more "oomph" but saves a lot of argument.

SWIFT RIVER
Sneaky surface-level rocks (opposite top) lurking inches above the water waiting to snag the unwary.

CRAFTSMANSHIP
For the dedicated racer and cruiser, the hours spent in the shop (opposite center) are as much a part of boating as those on the water.

CORRABASSET RIVER
Framed by gray birch (opposite bottom), open boaters maneuver down a Class-2 section. A touch of the blade in just the right place (below) can thread your boat through incredibly tight spots.

Allagash Waterway

CLASS: 1–2

DESCRIPTION: Large lakes and small ponds connected by narrow- to medium-width Allagash River; mostly flat, occasional brief rapids.

STANDARD RUN: Put in at Telos Lake, SE end of Chamberlain Lake on logging road; portage into Eagle Lake, then to Churchill Lake, then to Allagash Stream; 104 mi. to town of Allagash at confluence with St. John River. *Shorter run*—Put in at Cliff Lake or Umsaskis Lake. *Longer run*—Start Moosehead Lake to North Bay; 3 mi. portage NW to Black Pond, then to Caucomgomoc Lake; paddle N up Ciss Stream to Round Pond, then Poland Pond; another 3 mi. portage into Allagash Lake—the headwaters of the Allagash River; follow Allagash Stream into Chamberlain Lake and up to St. John confluence; total distance approx. 170 mi.

LOCATION: 3 hrs. NW of Bangor, Me.

RUNNING SEASON: Possible mid-May to mid-October; normally late June through August.

The very word Allagash conjures up visions of maple, moose, and the deep Maine woods. Visions of Indians deftly gliding bark canoes along a swift river and mighty loggers swinging double-bit axes into hundred-foot pole pines add romance to this unsullied, almost-wilderness waterway. The Allagash also conjures up visions of huge Class-10, boat-swamping rapids lying in wait around every corner. This is just not so.

There are innumerable trips of varying lengths possible on the Allagash Waterway. But no matter where the put-in and take-out are, most of the trip will be flat. The enormous lakes on the southern section (Chamberlain and Eagle) can become incredibly windy, and many boaters have been pinned down on islands overnight. After that, the Allagash becomes a chain alternating between river and small lakes.

The major rapids are the Chase Rip and the following seven miles of the Allagash Stream which start at Churchill Depot at the very end of Heron Lake. Depending on how much water you can persuade the ranger to release from the dam, the river flows from Class 1+ to a maximum of 2+. For the inexperienced, it is nerve wracking, though probably not dangerous. A path allows you to carry boats and/or gear around this entire section.

This is also an excellent trip for the wilderness paddler who has always spurned white water and the athlete who paddles purely for exercise. Anyone planning a trip here should write: Maine Forest Service, State Office, Augusta, Maine 04330.

The forest service requires anyone paddling in this region to register with it. This registration helps the gathering of statistics but, more importantly, puts a rescue team in your wake if you get lost. In addition, the park service informs you of strictly enforced regulations that insure the protection of this wilderness area.

A final note: Many guidebooks and pamphlets recommend Haymock Lake to Smith Brook as an Allagash put-in. Most of the year Smith Brook is reduced to a very small trickle of water. If you find yourself stuck in this bone-dry creek, follow the example of one party: Wade out and dam up Smith Brook with dead logs and stone; pray for a thunderstorm during the night. Then, if your prayers have been answered, you will be able to break the dam in the morning and follow that first flood right into the Allagash.

ALLAGASH WATERWAY
Maine holds some of the broadest and longest whitewater rivers in the Northeast.
Two paddlers (opposite) having just finished the carry, sit and watch the Allagash Falls.

Androscoggin River

CLASS: 3

DESCRIPTION: Broad, rocky, somewhat shallow; long continuous rapids followed by long flat stretches.

STANDARD RUN: Put in at Erroll, N.H., below Erroll Dam; 10 mi. to Seven Island Bridge or put in at Pontook Dam, run 3 mi. to Dummer.

LOCATION: 4½ hrs. N of Boston; above White Mountain Natl. Forest, W of Rangely Lakes.

RUNNING SEASON: June through mid-October; occasionally earlier with water releases (call (207) 784-4501 for info.).

If you are not quite ready for the Rapid River but you still want some midsummer white water in the same White Mountain scenery, drive a few miles west to the Androscoggin. Between Erroll, the traditional Rangely Lakes take-out, and Berlin, thirty-five miles downstream, there flow long stretches of water to challenge every level of boater. If you are just starting out and are wary of biting off too much, your best bet is to scout out a section by car; Route 16 follows the entire river to Berlin.

If you can competently handle Class-3 water, put in at Erroll. The first mile-and-a-half section is a continuous boulder field. Irregular and jarring haystacks make this an ideal place to swamp an open boat. In addition, the river is just broad and rocky enough so that you can sink on your way to a shore eddy. Then, after three or four miles of flat water which loops through a pine and maple forest, a series of tight, rocky, pool-and-plunge rapids begins. These blind-corner ledges eventually ease off into a steady current that runs swiftly over some small rock gardens all the way down to the take-out.

If you are experienced and have saved a little energy, treat yourself to the two continuous miles of Class 3 below the Pontook dam. It is tricky reading the water, and a bowman who is not alert can lead you down an ever-narrowing channel to an almost certain broach. Playing souseholes is not a frequent option on the Androscoggin, but for a paddler with any experience who wants to spin in midriver eddies and hone down his slalom reflexes, this river has the rapids that will keep him working.

ANDROSCOGGIN RIVER
*John Berry, one of the best, wields his old model
C-1 downstream towards the next slalom gate. At this
time the C-1 still retained a classic canoe shape.*

West River

CLASS: 3

DESCRIPTION: Swift, continuous, narrow but widening; usually open with some ledges and boulder gardens.

STANDARD RUN: Put in at Ball Mountain Dam, Vt. (Jamaica State Park); 6 mi. to Townsend Dam.

LOCATION: 3 hrs. NW of Boston; 2 hrs. S of Montpelier, Vt.

RUNNING SEASON: Late March through June; occasional water releases in summer and fall.

All of about a decade ago when an open Grumman could still place in the C-2 class and C-1s were called banana boats, the West River was the traditional site of the National Slalom Championships. Boat designs and paddling techniques have changed since then, but the West still offers a swift challenge to open boaters and an interesting playing course for the "men in fiber glass."

The run starts from the bottom of Ball Mountain Dam where the river is fifty feet at its widest and twists over a staircase of small ledges that demand much zigzagging. (Local paddlers say that if you can make the put-in, you can paddle the river. Rocks and gaping potholes can make the dirt road leading to the water a wet portage. The scramble down the over-the-dam can do more damage than any rapid.)

The real boat-cruncher on the West is the Dumplings. Most of the river flows into these three truck-size boulders in a single tongue of white. The trick is to adjust to the sudden acceleration of this chute and make an almost right-angle turn without scraping a head-high boulder.

Salmon Hole, the midway point located in Jamaica State Park, interrupts the almost continuous Class-3 run from the dam and marks the site of the old National Slalom course. It is an excellent place to beach, have lunch, and wander through the thick pine forests.

Paddling to the Townsend Reservoir, the stream broadens and the steep staircases turn into open boulder fields. These Class-2+ rapids offer ample space for the open boater and closed boater to play. Despite its lack of accessibility, the West remains one of the most popular whitewater rivers in Vermont.

WEST RIVER
*But today the C-1 has lowered both its ends
and its volume to make it sleeker, more maneuverable,
and scarcely discernible from a kayak.*

Hudson River

CLASS: 3–4

DESCRIPTION: Deep, wide, powerful river; long boulder patches—swift, flat sections.

STANDARD RUN: Put in from the dirt road off Rte. 28, 1 mi. E of Indian Lake, N.Y., along Indian Creek (Hudson tributary); 16 mi. to North River, N.Y., also on Rte. 28; 6 mi. to North Creek, N.Y.; 10 mi. from North Creek to The Glen, N.Y.

LOCATION: 4 hrs. directly N of New York City; 4½ hrs. NW of Boston.

RUNNING SEASON: Late March to mid-June.

Rapids? On the Hudson? To most New Yorkers the concept seems as incongruous as an elephant in running shoes. But the Hudson is not always the sleepy giant that lumbers through the Palisades into New York Harbor. Two hundred miles upriver it is an aggressive Adirondack stream, fast flowing and constantly enlarged by hundreds of little feeder streams.

From Indian Creek to North River the Hudson pushes its way through a steep-sided rocky gorge over mile-long boulder fields, creating some fascinating, if risky, play spots. Between these large rock gardens, occasional ledges and boulder piles funnel the river into steep, sudden drops. Blue Ledge, a prime example, has dumped many a victim.

Coming out of the gorge at the Boreas confluence, the river quickly widens beyond stone's-throw width, but the same steady gradient keeps it always moving, even in the flat stretches. In March and April, spring flood waters surge down the Hudson and raise it to decked-boat-only levels, and a good thunderstorm can repeat that performance even in late May. But the level tends to drop quickly, and by summer the river holds more rocks than allure.

Along the gorge and all the way to Gooley Glen, one is struck by the lush Adirondack woodlands. Huge white birch stand tall among the hemlock, maple, and occasional oaks. Many boaters prefer to make a weekend trip running from the Indian to North Creek just for the experience of camping overnight in the dense wild forest that lines the steep granite gorge.

One final note about the Hudson River: While not exactly thrilling white water, one of the most fascinating canoe trips the metropolitan canoer can make is to paddle around his own Manhattan Island. It's thirty-five miles, but if you figure the tides correctly, it can be done without *too* much difficulty in a single day.

DEAD RIVER
Although the wooden pole (below) seems an outdated tool for the fiberglass kayak, the combination works well on the shallow rivers of the Northeast.

CROOKED RIVER
(opposite) *Northeast paddlers catch some of the best white water in early March, when plenty of snow remains on the banks and bodies are drenched by thirty-four degree water.*

Shepaug River

CLASS: 2–2+

DESCRIPTION: Narrow, rocky, shallow; short rapids and shoals interspersed with short flat stretches.

STANDARD RUN: Put in at Washington Depot Bridge (Rte. 47); 8 mi. to Judd's Bridge or (2+) put in at Bantam Lake; 7 mi. to Washington Depot.

LOCATION: 1 hr. W of Hartford, Conn.

RUNNING SEASON: Late February to mid-April.

It is early March. You have just gotten a phone call telling you the ice has broken, and it is time to struggle into your wet suit and hit the Shepaug. Arriving at the put-in, all those first-of-season trepidations come back. The snow is a foot high on the banks, someone has measured the water temperature at thirty-seven degrees, and you never quite got around to those midwinter workouts. . . . But in you go just the same.

For an initial cruise the Shepaug is an excellent river. This rocky, narrow little stream boasts enough current to bring back the exhilaration of white water but not the kind of difficulty that will plunge you inexorably into a keeper hole at your first mistake. The rapids are mostly easy-to-read tongues of water working their way through short, technical rock gardens, and a few drops that seem custom-made for practicing eddy turns and ferrying. It is a fun river for making your own slalom course with lots of small vest-pocket side eddies where you can spin and run backwards.

For the novice it is an ideal place to learn with a mentor. The short rapids followed by the never-too-long flat pools give the paddler a feeling that a rest is never too far off. The best novice run is Washington Depot to Judd's Bridge. For those looking for a tighter, more challenging trip, try putting in on Bantam Lake and running down to Washington Depot.

During its brief season the canoeist catches the narrow Shepaug Valley at its most lovely. Thickly wooded banks slant steeply down to the water's edge. The boater who paddles through this forest just after a fresh snowfall is greeted by an awesome beauty that more than compensates for the March chill. Paddling under snow-laden arches of young saplings bent low over the river is one of the river runner's exclusive joys that brings him back to a world from which too many have drifted away.

Moose River

CLASS: 2+ −4

DESCRIPTION: Groups of ledges and tight, forceful chutes, broken by long stretches of flat water; medium width but often constricted and rocky.

STANDARD RUN: Put in below dam at Minnehaha, N.Y. (middle branch); 7 mi. to McKeever (just below confluence with southern branch). *Longer run*—Put in at Thendara, paddle 8 mi. to Minnehaha.

LOCATION: 1 hr. N of Utica; just W of Adirondacks.

RUNNING SEASON: March through May; September to November; occasional late spring and summer releases.

When you are popping enders in your T-shirt at Nantahala or charging down Idaho's Hell's Canyon in mid-August, it is very easy to sneer at the Old New England Reserve. But if your season starts in February in the middle of the northern snowbelt, and if you put in with ice on the eddies and drifts on the banks, and the first Eskimo roll makes you literally see stars, then maybe New Englander hesitation is more a matter of survival than cowardice.

If you are still not convinced, try the Moose the weekend after the ice breaks. With surprising surges of power this river twists its way through boulder-choked chutes and over triple-drop staircases, all demanding quick reactions or a chilly punishment. A typical run on the Moose is a paddle along a few hundred yards of flat water until the river suddenly drops from in front of you. You quickly pick a slot on the left and drop over the ledge. Then you zig to the right and zag to the left for the next two ledges. After these drops the rapid slows up through a technical rock garden.

An open boater's favorite, the Moose was the site of the 1975 Open Nationals and countless other slalom and downriver races. The tight turns on the ledges of this stream can make it a real boat-cruncher, but not a people-eater. Most of the rapids are Class 2+−3+ with a few Class-4 drops. But water level means everything on this river and, since it is dam controlled, it can rise as much as three feet during a run.

If you are having trouble in the first half, be sure to take out before McKeever. After that the road leaves the river and it is a tough scramble out when you have left your boat wrapped at Wishbone or Mixmaster. But if you have the experience and you have checked the water level, don't miss the Moose. It offers the thrill of technical rock dodging on a powerful stream in the beautiful and remote Adirondack region.

Housatonic River

CLASS: 1+ to West Cornwall Bridge; 3 below Bulls Bridge

DESCRIPTION: Medium width, shoaly, small rocks, shallow, constant current.

STANDARD RUN: 1+—Put in at Falls Village, Conn.; 10 mi. to West Cornwall bridge. 3—Bulls Bridge, 5 mi. to Kent, Conn.

LOCATION: 1 hr. W of Hartford, Conn.

RUNNING SEASON: Late February to early April. Occasional late spring and fall water releases.

For those who want to believe that New England hasn't been entirely developed by urban sprawl and vast tracts of aluminum condominiums, a trip down the Housatonic will restore their faith. Romantic little towns still separate the long stretches of pine forests. Covered bridges span the river at Gaylordsville and Cornwall Bridge. Although civilization has crept in, very little of the charm is gone.

The river, small at Falls Village, grows steadily wider, but it remains shallow, even in early spring. The current is slow but relatively constant for Class 1+. As in most of Connecticut, rocks are everywhere. A sudden pitch in the gradient can turn the whole river into a shoal. It is not uncommon to see a novice bowman on The Hoose frantically screaming, "Left; no, right; I mean left!" while a muddled sternman struggles to obey all three commands simultaneously, and the boat, left to itself, gently settles on top of a large rock—or two.

But for those who have mastered even the most basic whitewater techniques, the Housatonic makes a lovely cruise and excellent training ground. There is enough current to give the beginner the feel of moving water but not enough to spill him every time he makes a wrong wriggle.

The five miles from Bulls Bridge down is another story. This short run is a gathering place for experienced paddlers of all types. For the cruiser there is a continuous series of Class−2−2+ rock dodging spiced with granite ledges that form some tricky Class-3 drops. For the hotdogger, heaven is here. The curlers and holes formed by these ledges are excellent sites for pop-ups, enders, spins, and the whole array of stunts available to the expert.

If you are a kibitzer, the Housatonic is a good bet. Route 7 follows the entire river. Or if you tire of watching the crazies have all the fun, the old stone inns around Lake Waramaug or towns such as New Milford are easy to find and explore.

EAST BRANCH—PENOBSCOT RIVER
*Open-boat wildwater racers (above) charge
downstream, trying to ship as little water as possible
while maintaining maximum speed in the rapids.*

WEST BRANCH—PENOBSCOT RIVER
A solo paddler (below) easily negotiates a Class-2 drop.

Westfield River—North Branch

CLASS: 3+

DESCRIPTION: Broad, swift, continuous; boulder gardens with occasional drops.

STANDARD RUN: Put in below Knightsville Dam off Rte. 112; 6 mi. to Huntington; take-out at dam by Rte. 20.

LOCATION: 45 min. W of Springfield, Mass.

RUNNING SEASON: March to June; occasional fall water releases.

You are ready for some heavier water, but you do not want to drive five hours just to find that the water is beyond you and end up running shuttle for the others all weekend. This is the problem faced by all intermediate paddlers, and in Massachusetts the Westfield River provides an answer.

Between the west, middle, and north branches of the Westfield there are over half a dozen day-long trips ranging from beginner's training runs right up to Class 4. In addition, you can scout all of the middle and much of the west and north branches by road. Check with local clubs and you are bound to find some section that is challenging and still manageable.

Some of the most exciting rapids flow from the Knightsville dam to the confluence of the three branches just below Huntington—a popular race course. The rapids consist mainly of chair- and car-size boulders that divert the broad river into several channels. It does not look overly technical, but a deceptively swift current demands some split-second reactions. Just before the middle branch enters from the right lies The Gorge, a mile-long heavy-water boulder field, climaxing in a three-foot ledge across the entire river. A steep chute funnels you down into a rolling curler that loves to swamp Grummans and roll slow-moving kayaks.

The rapids are long, but there are pools where you can sigh with relief—and bail. The Westfield is a river that takes some planning and water-reading to select the right channel. But for the intermediate paddler who is ready to try both heavy water and technical rock dodging, this river makes an exhilarating run.

Farmington River

CLASS: (2) to Tariffville; (4) to New Boston

DESCRIPTION: (2)—Many small rocks and shoals; short rapids; one big broken dam. (4)—Very narrow, tight; very rocky; strong continuous current; few eddies.

STANDARD RUN: (2)—Put in at Granby, Conn., 6 mi. to Tariffville. (4)—Put in at Otis, Mass., 8 mi. to New Boston; 4 more mi. to Colebrook Reservoir.

LOCATION: Crosses Mass./Conn. border; 1 hr. W of Springfield, Mass.

RUNNING SEASON: March to early May; then late September to early November.

This narrow little stream demands more rock dodging per mile than just about any river in New England. A surprisingly heavy volume of water rushes over a garden of jagged rocks in a riverbed that frequently narrows to the width of a gully. For most of the New Boston section, the rapids run continuously, broken only by occasional stretches of flat water, allowing the paddler to catch a quick breath between drops. There are a few eddies where you can stop and play, but generally there is a single narrow channel with just enough room to make it through. Finding the one access demands all your technical skill and quick reflexes.

Since there is so little room in which to play and the current is so swift, the Otis-to-New Boston run can be made two or three times a day. Many boaters start at the Slalom Course Bridge (three miles downstream of Otis) and run downstream five miles to experience the most exciting part of the river. A road follows the river the entire trip, and the steep, although not very high, banks provide excellent vantage points. This is not only convenient for paddlers spotting cars and making rescues, but if you are a spectator wanting a good firsthand look at the sport, you can follow a group all the way down the river.

Wider, shallower, and less rocky than the New Boston run, the six miles from Granby to Tariffville make an excellent Class-2 training run. The rocks are small and far enough apart, and they can be easily bypassed by boaters who have mastered the basic skills. In a few sections, shoals and constricted banks form short series of foot-high standing waves.

But the best memories of this part of the Farmington come from the broken dam at Tariffville. The entire river funnels through a narrow slit and drops four feet into a mass of foam, haystacks, and shifting current. Swamping is easy and portaging may be wise. But the neophyte who completes this rapid upright gets a short, sweet glimpse of all the wildwater thrill that lies ahead.

BALANCE
The two paddlers (opposite) are trying valiantly to stay upright—and are apparently succeeding.

SWIFT RIVER
Paddlers (opposite top) skirt the foaming hole on their right and cling to a dark, smooth tongue of water.

BREAKFAST
The aluminum groaning board (opposite center) made from a much-scarred overturned canoe is a handy table for the sunrise meal.

PEELING OUT
The current slams the upturned hull of a racer (opposite bottom), who rejoins the mainstream after negotiating the slalom gate in the eddy behind him.

WINTER
Cold weather paddlers (below) shoot a broken dam and bury the bow in a foaming roller caused by the drop and cross-currents.

Esopus River

CLASS: 3

DESCRIPTION: Narrow, rocky, swift, continuous; deceptively difficult.

STANDARD RUN: Put in at The Portal between Allaben and Phonecia (Rte. 28); 12 mi. to Boiceville.

LOCATION: 2 hrs. N of New York City.

RUNNING SEASON: March through mid-June; very occasional water releases in summer.

There is probably more aluminum wrapped around the rocks of the Esopus than any other river in this region. It is a boat salvager's delight, not because it rivals the Grand Canyon in power but because it is a popular proving ground for those making the big step from Class 2 to Class 3.

This narrow little river has a surprisingly strong current that flows continuously, caroming from bank to bank for the first four miles. It is a fairly steep, swift sleigh ride with just enough rocks and fallen trees to keep you thinking. Toward the end, the river broadens and becomes a series of ledges and shoals separated by long flat stretches.

But in between these two sections comes the river's real challenge. For about half a mile a swift, powerful current races over two boulder fields called Railroad and Elmer's Diner Rapids. One of the more popular ways to run Railroad Rapids is to panic at this rushing sea of white, paddle like crazy, and scream bloody murder at your bowman as the water pours in over his lap and your boat sinks like a stone. A dryer, albeit less daring, method is to pull into the eddy on the right, scout the rapid thoroughly from the railroad tracks, then backpaddle through it with the bowman kneeling behind the bow seat. After carrying back up and running Railroad two or three more times, you head downstream for Elmer's, where you are slightly less likely to swamp in high waves but more likely to broach on a boulder.

It is an excellent river for the spectator: Three races are run here every year, and all can be seen from the open shoreline along Railroad Rapids. If you are trying to decide on a new boat, or just seeking new paddling partners, come to the Esopus the first weekend in June and you'll find advice, bargains, and friends in abundance.

THE DROP AND THE DUMP
*The bowman wisely moved aft to avoid shipping
water over the bow on this drop. Unfortunately, balance
still needs just a touch of work.*

Beaverkill River

CLASS: 1 + –2

DESCRIPTION: Ever broadening; winding; swift, swirly water; almost continuous current.

STANDARD RUN: Put in at or just above Beaverkill Campground NE of Roscoe; 14 mi. to Butternut Campground, just past town of Cooks Falls; 10 more mi. to confluence with east branch of Delaware River.

LOCATION: 3 hrs. NW of New York City just off Rte. 17.

RUNNING SEASON: Early March to late May.

On the bridge high above the foaming rapids of Cooks Falls, a passerby dressed in winter clothing paused by the railing. He stared down at a young girl swimming valiantly across the current toward shore. In a moment of bravery our Galahad leaped from the bridge into the icy March water. Coming up from behind, he deftly seized the swimmer by the throat and screamed, "I've got you, I've got you!" Our damsel, a wet-suited expert who had just dumped her kayak, shouted back, "Well get your #$%&#+! hands off me and grab my boat!"

Unfortunately, we cannot claim that every Beaverkill paddler will have this exciting a trip, but for the novice wanting to test his blade against a faster current, this is the river. From the put-in the river flows swiftly through constricting shoals and a sprinkling of rocks. A series of tight S-turns backs up the current, making for surprisingly bouncy haystacks on the outside of the curves.

At the confluence with the Willowemoc, about halfway down the run, the river makes a ninety-degree right-hand turn. As in several other places, the riverbed here is marshy, and at high water it floods the forest. It is very tempting to paddle in and out of the trees, but it is also the surest way to pin both yourself and your boat underwater. Once you have seen a friend held under by a tree branch, you will realize that oak can be more vicious than granite.

Under the Route 17 bridges the water constricts into boiling eddies, but the major Beaverkill rapids are at Cooks Falls. These several hundred yards of continuous drop demand some sharp boulder weaving, and for the experienced wave surfer it is a marvelous playground. The Beaverkill is one of the bouncy little rivers that was designed to give confidence to the first-season paddler and plant a restlessness for something bigger.

SACO RIVER
Choosing the right tongue is everything in boat control. The theory is that the water always takes you where you want to go. All you have to do is avoid the rocks.

MIDDLE ATLANTIC

The Mid-Atlantic stands as a region of transition between the boulder-choked, low-volume streams of New England and the larger, more open rivers of the Southeast. As a result, its rivers contain elements of both. In New Jersey streams are many but white water is scarce. These stretches are short, winding, and must be caught right after a heavy rain. The shallow water presents a maze of surface rocks. Northern Pennsylvania contains rivers of varying size, but they tend to be rocky and technical. Typically, vertical drops and small boulder patches alternate with flat pools. Moving south, the rivers tend to be fuller and the white water on a larger, less technical scale. Holes and hydraulics mix equally with rock gardens.

By West Virginia, you've reached big water country. Small technical rivers still abound but tend to flow into larger, somewhat more open rivers, where technical ability must be accompanied by heavy water skills, and muscling the river is out of the question.

Normally, the spring thaw comes in early March with snowmelt and rains maintaining high levels through mid- or late June. Summer is dry, except for a few larger, dam-controlled rivers. From mid-September through November, sporadic but heavy rains raise the rivers again in some areas. But the water levels of this region in no way reflect the paddling season. The devoted have their boats in the water every weekend from March first to Thanksgiving. They think nothing of traveling ten hours north or south during the summer to find a good river with a dam release.

Some of the most avid race training goes on in the Mid-Atlantic, and legions of paddlers follow the eastern racing circuit every weekend, competing in the Northeast and Southeast as well as in their own region.

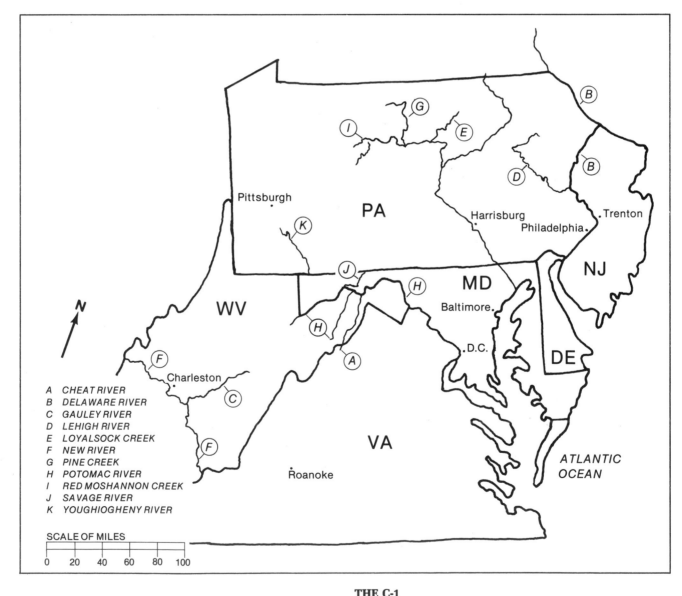

A   CHEAT RIVER
B   DELAWARE RIVER
C   GAULEY RIVER
D   LEHIGH RIVER
E   LOYALSOCK CREEK
F   NEW RIVER
G   PINE CREEK
H   POTOMAC RIVER
I   RED MOSHANNON CREEK
J   SAVAGE RIVER
K   YOUGHIOGHENY RIVER

SCALE OF MILES

0   20   40   60   80   100

THE C-1
Popular particularly among Eastern, heavy-water paddlers, the single-man decked canoe (opposite) has all the capabilities of the kayak while affording the familiar kneeling position and single blade of canoeing.

YOUGHIOGHENY RIVER
*Paddlers get set (above) for Railroad Rapids immediately
downstream. In summer and early fall the level drops,
making the Yough a great open-boat stream.*

SPEED
*A wildwater kayak (below) slashes through
sun-sparkling waters. These narrow craft are tough to
balance and maneuver but are oh-so-fast on the
straightaway.*

Delaware River

CLASS: 1 +

DESCRIPTION: Very large, wide, slow moving; long flat stretches broken by short rapids.

STANDARD RUN: Put in at Callicoon, N.Y.; 12 mi. to Narrowsburg, 12 mi. more to Minisink Ford, 18 mi. more to Port Jervis.

STANDARD RUN: Put in at Dingmans Ferry, Pa.; 27 mi. to Delaware Water Gap.

LOCATION: 1¼–2 hrs. NW of New York, N.Y.

RUNNING SEASON: *All* year.

In 1795 ox teams dragged six eighty-foot pole pines from the little settlement of Mast Hope down to the Delaware River. These specially cut logs were floated downstream, then up to Boston to become masts for the *U.S.S. Constitution*—"Old Ironsides." Today, little Mast Hope still stands on the Delaware, but the lumbermen and log rafts have yielded to paddlers seeking their first taste of whitewater.

After you have served your flat-water apprenticeship, this river is an excellent choice for your whitewater baptism. From Deposit, New York, down 150 miles to Easton, Pennsylvania, the boater can find enjoyable riffles and Class-1 rapids, spiced with an occasional Class-2 section. Dumping on a river as broad as the Delaware can mean a very long swim with your boat before you reach shore. But most rapids consist of a swift current and standing waves. Rocks exist, but they are easily spotted and are not too numerous. As on all large rivers, a single downed tree or huge boulder will not make any passage terribly treacherous.

Stories are told of vast hordes descending on Callicoon, Narrowsburg, Dingmans Ferry, and other towns where the unprepared venture into the uncalculated. While the hordes may be real at the put-in, they tend to dissipate on the river, and paddling through the pine forests and pastureland of the broad Delaware Valley can be enjoyably scenic, even if it is not completely remote. You lose this semisolitary feeling only at the major rapids— particularly Skinners Falls, Shohola, Mongaup, and Foul Rift. Here boaters gather to run the "tougher stuff" over and over. If you spill, you may be mighty glad of that stranger's helping hand that gets you and your craft out quickly.

The best possible way to paddle the Delaware is to carry your gear and camp along the riverbank. Local outfitters will help plan a trip based on your skill and give you a map of shoreline campsites. For hundred-mile expeditions or training all day at a single rapid, such as Foul Rift, this river provides an excellent entry into year-round whitewater.

Lehigh River

CLASS: 2 + –3 +

DESCRIPTION: Relatively wide; boulder patches of varying lengths interspersed with long, slow stretches of flat water.

STANDARD RUN: Put in at White Haven, Pa., directly off Rte. 80; 11 mi. to Rockport, 14 mi. more to Jim Thorpe.

LOCATION: 1 hr. S of Scranton, Pa.; 2 hrs. W of New York, N.Y.

RUNNING SEASON: March through June; occasional weekend water releases throughout summer and fall.

So you want to play, hmm? You're no great hot-dogger, but you still want to try out some snap eddy turns and wave surfing in a powerful and sometimes tricky current. The Lehigh is your river. Flowing over a broad bed of chair-size boulders, the river provides a natural slalom course, challenging to cruise through and exciting to play in.

At most times of year, the Lehigh offers the intermediate a happy balance between tight, technical rock dodging and heavy water surviving. Like most large, rock-filled rivers, it's not overly swift but is deceptively powerful. For many an eastern boater, this is the first step up from Class-2 water. All of a sudden the paddler clashes head on with a powerful lengthy rapid like the Eighty-foot Mile—something he just can't muscle his way out of. If he's wise, he will take it slowly and struggle to use the current. If he's pigheaded, he'll fight it and end up hiking out along the Lehigh Railroad tracks, leaving his boat wrapped around a rock and his gear floating downriver. But for those with experience, the Lehigh is an enjoyable challenge. Strong paddlers make the entire twenty-five-mile run from White Haven to Jim Thorpe in a single day. Those wanting a more leisurely trip, with more playing time, take a full weekend, camping anywhere along the left bank. The valley walls are steep and thickly wooded, but there is ample room close to the shore.

A note to the heavy-water paddler: The Lehigh is dam controlled and normally flows 700 to 1,300 cfs throughout the spring. However, there are frequent water releases from the upstream reservoir, raising the level to as much as 4,000 cfs. Generally releases are on weekends and local clubs have a schedule. It's worth checking. When the dam dumps water, the Lehigh becomes a different river, and those boulder fields are covered over by huge standing waves, swift tongues, and souseholes—all making for a great sleigh ride.

Loyalsock Creek

CLASS: 3+ –4+

DESCRIPTION: Powerful, tricky water; long boulder fields, many drops; short pools.

STANDARD RUN: Put in at bridge on Rte. 220, Pa.; 9 mi. to World's End State Park. *Possible with high water:* Put in at Lopez; 8 mi. to Rte. 220 bridge.

LOCATION: 1 hr. W of Scranton, Pa.; 4½ hrs. W of New York, N.Y.

RUNNING SEASON: Late February to mid-May.

Friday morning, this "river" may be little more than a narrow trickle through a mass of car-size boulders. But a short thunderstorm can raise the river level as much as two feet and keep it up for a 4+ run on Saturday. Few rivers in the East respond to rain as quickly or drastically as the Loyalsock.

The Loyalsock pounds its way powerfully and almost continuously from Route 220 to a large pool and a three-foot dam in World's End State Park. Along its narrow twisting course, huge boulders form keeper holes and tight, steeply dropping chutes. Throughout this high-speed, rock-dodging run, the paddler is constantly hanging on a draw or pry.

For the very experienced the Loyalsock is a tooth-jarring challenge. For the neophyte it is sheer insanity. This is a dangerous river: Pools are rare and eddies are small and tricky to hit. Hemlock logs frequently fall across the only available channel. The holes are easy to fall into, tricky to get out of, and they dump you on a rock rather than in a flat pool. The incredibly swift water fluctuation can turn yesterday's sleigh ride into today's deathtrap. Add to this a river bed that is constantly twisting around a blind corner through a remote wooded canyon, and you have one hell of a hard day's work.

Get out and scout this one every so often, even if you have run it before. You can't hotdog your way through a downed tree. There are many rivers tougher to run than this one, but few are so unforgiving and exact so strict a penalty for a missed stroke or poor judgment.

The run from Lopez to Route 220 is generally considered the limit for open boats with one ledge that most open experts carry around. It's heavy, tight, exhilarating water. If the water level floods out your plans for the upper and lower level, you can run from World's End State Park three miles down to Forksville, a Class-1-to-2 run, then spend Sunday hiking along the Loyalsock Trail, which provides magnificent vistas of the river from atop the canyon.

THE ESKIMO ROLL

Sometimes a convenience, sometimes a safety measure. When overturned, the paddler swings self and boat upright, using hips and blade. It takes practice but can save you a long swim.

1975 NATIONAL CHAMPIONSHIP
Paddlers work to negotiate the red-and-white striped
poles. Unlike slalom in skiing, you can't touch them. The
K-1 (below) turns in the fastest times, while the C-2
(above) turns in the slowest.

Pine Creek

CLASS: 1+–2

DESCRIPTION: Narrow to medium width; shallow and shoals; quick short rapids separate long stretches of flat water.

STANDARD RUN: Put in at Ansonia, Pa.; 15 mi. to Blackwell, 3 mi. more to Cedar Run, 4 mi. more to Slate Run.

LOCATION: 2½ hrs. N of Harrisburg, Pa.; 5½ hrs. W of New York City.

RUNNING SEASON: March through May.

Pine Creek passes through the "Grand Canyon of Pennsylvania" and is worth paddling for the view alone. Steep cliffs of granite tower over a thousand feet above the shoreline. Beech, hemlock, and maple grow out at impossible angles and fur the stone walls with green. All this foliage covering a "canyon" is often more than a little boggling to westerners. To the Arizonan a canyon is new, bare rock with a few patches of dirt clinging to the crevices. But "out East," where mountains are older and soil is deeper, flora covers even the steepest slopes.

For the whitewater novice Pine Creek is an interesting, if long, trip. The first fifteen miles to Blackwell consists primarily of shallow, medium-length rock gardens separated by long stretches of flat water. But fortunately the stream constricts in several places forming narrow, powerful jets that sweep the paddler around the corners. From Blackwell to Slate Run the river picks up steam and becomes a solid Class 2. A more powerful current makes eddies more prominent and the stream more playable.

For the paddling camper Pine Creek is a good weekend bet. You can pull right off the river and camp at Blackwell (unfortunately not before), and the short seven miles to Slate Run the next day gets you off the river early and heading for home well before dark. Pine Creek is also popular with expedition paddlers who continue for another forty miles to its confluence with the Susquehanna.

WEST BRANCH—SUSQUEHANNA RIVER
The sun sparkles on the surface obscuring the rocks as a paddler maneuvers his way through a Class-1+ stretch of shallow water.

Red Moshannon Creek

CLASS: 2–2+

DESCRIPTION: Shallow, twisty, but broad; rock gardens and chutes alternate with medium-length flat stretches.

STANDARD RUN: Put in near jct. Rte. 80 (in Pa.); 7 mi. to Rte. 53 (confluence with Black Moshannon Creek).

LOCATION: 2½ hrs. NE of Pittsburgh, Pa.; 45 min. NW of State College, Pa.

RUNNING SEASON: Late February to June.

For the Class-2 paddler, the "Red Mo" offers some sporty chutes and rock dodging in a current that gradually gains power and acceleration. This river, along with its more challenging Class-3+ neighbor, the "Black Mo," forms the mainstream for hundreds of little feeder tributaries that trickle off the foothills of the Appalachians and the Alleghenies, where they join in central Pennsylvania.

Local open and closed boaters often cruise this river as a spring warm-up or when everything else nearby has run dry. If you are not from the area, beware of the Red Mo in early spring. It flows through a steep, wooded valley where the last of the damp morning mist spirals out at noon and re-descends at 4:00 P.M. This much humidity greatly increases the danger of hypothermia.

The rapids start out as shoals of varying lengths, with the river rippling over little fist-size rocks and then landing on a flat stretch. As the water gets deeper, the rocks grow bigger, forming boulder-pile ledges and tight little drops. Many of these chutes are excellent for snap eddy turns, but wave surfing requires a good rainfall.

The Red Mo is one of those relatively out-of-the-way rivers that offers a real allure for the paddler who likes alternately to hike and canoe. Good trails can be found along the dirt road which follows river on the left, or in nearby Black Moshannon State Park. The hardy bushwacker who wants to scout a more technical and interesting river can start hiking at the Red Moshannonnan Creek takeout by the Rte. 53 Bridge, and follow the Black Moshannon Creek upstream from where it flows in on the right.

POTOMAC RIVER
The high kneeling position is standard in flatwater racing. It provides extra power but sacrifices control. Whitewater racers will often revert to this on flat stretches.

Youghiogheny River

CLASS: 3–4

DESCRIPTION: Broad powerful river with short, very playable rapids. Basically pool-and-plunge with many holes and trails of haystacks.

STANDARD RUN: Put in at Ohiopyle State Park, Pa.; 11 mi. to Connellsville.

LOCATION: 1 hr. SE of Pittsburgh, Pa.

RUNNING SEASON: Class 4 from March to mid-June; lower water Class 3 until November.

Legend has it that God created the Yough in answer to a paddler's prayer. For the experienced white-water boater, this broad, beautifully scenic river has it all and has it longer than any river in the area. The short, dramatic rapids offer a smorgasbord of whitewater challenge: steep ledges, bouncy sleigh rides in heavy water, and tight technical maneuvering through boulder patches. These tough sections are conveniently interspersed with calm pools, where the boater can stop and collect his wits—along with gear, paddle, and boat if necessary.

The Yough is a high-volume river, and most of the rapids contain several possible channels, all filtering down to a flat pool. This seemingly inexhaustible variety makes the Youghiogheny a favorite stomping ground for hotdoggers, spinning in river currents and souseholes, putting their craft into nearly impossible places. Swimmers' Rapid, an excellent spot to lunch, swim, and play—or watch, boasts a huge, frothy curler that real experts bounce in and out of—without a paddle.

For the average river runner, who seeks merely to survive upright, this river offers more advantages than variety and easy rescue. In the droughts of August, when all the raging spring runoff has slowed to a trickle, Class-3+ whitewater still flows through the Yough. An eight-month running season makes boaters flock to the "only game in town" all summer long. In addition, from Memorial Day to Labor Day, hordes of rafters swell the river guided by local commercial outfitters. These big, black, moving rocks can prove quite a hazard for the inexperienced, but a spirit of cooperation pervades and the river is wide enough to accommodate all.

No one should paddle this river with blinders on. The Youghiogheny River flows through a sloping canyon covered with pine and hemlock. It is typical of the thick forest area that once covered the entire East Coast. At the end of the Loop, a two-mile oxbow that finishes one-eighth mile from the put-in, the boater can hike a hidden trail to Falling Water, the architectural marvel designed by Frank Lloyd Wright in 1933.

The Yough is worth running at any time of year, and don't be put off by tales of huge crowds. The feeling of being in a remote wilderness may have faded but the thrill and challenge of the river are as strong as ever.

YOUGHIOGHENY RIVER
A K-1W (woman kayakist) blasts her way through a hole. To the deep regret of the male chauvinist, women's times on the race course are only slightly above men's.

Potomac River

CLASS: 2–3
DESCRIPTION: Rocky, narrow, forceful; long rock gardens with short sections of flat water.
STANDARD RUN: Put in just below Mouth of Seneca, W.Va. along Rte. 28; 7 mi. to Smoke Hole Canyons (take-out parking by gift shop).
LOCATION: 1½ hrs. W of Washington, D.C.
RUNNING SEASON: Mid-March through May.

Enfolded in the steep hills of West Virginia, through a little valley choked with maple and oak, flows the "Petersburg" section of the South Branch of the Potomac. The first weekend in April, this sparsely populated valley springs to life in an April Fools' Festival, which includes the Mid-Atlantic Divisional race for canoe and kayak and the jovial "Anything that-Floats-but-is-not-a-Boat Race."

The Potomac at this point presents an interesting intermediate challenge offering a step up for the Class-2 paddler and familiar exhilaration for the Class-3. The rapids are long, powerful shoals sprinkled with just enough boulders to make the going technically difficult. A steep gradient and narrowing banks give this shallow river a deceptive speed. The flat stretches are of medium length, but they are infrequent enough to give the boater a feeling of continuous action.

The most frequent tales of the "Petersburg" center around Slide Rapids, a right-angle turn in the current that demands that the boater follow suit or else slam bow first into a large boulder.

For the novice there is a Class-1 + -to-2 run, which starts eleven miles above Petersburg on Route 220 and flows down to the put-in. Another event for the would-be whitewater paddler is Wildwater Fair at the April Fools' Festival. Held Saturday night between races, the fair is attended by all major equipment manufacturers. For the paddler it offers a place to sell, buy, or find boats, blades, duct tape, clubs, paddling partners, and endless diatribes on technique. Even if you don't race, it is an event not to be missed.

TEAMWORK
Competitors watch from below as the bow paddler draws the bow past a ledge and the sternman powers his end out of a hole.

Savage River

CLASS: 4

DESCRIPTION: Swift, continuously rocky; heavy volume, narrow streambed; constant turns.

STANDARD RUN: Put in below dam at Savage River State Park, Md.; 6 mi. to Piedmont.

LOCATION: 2½ hrs. NW of Washington, D.C.; 25 mi. SW of Cumberland, Md.

RUNNING SEASON: March through May, depending upon water releases; occasional June releases.

If you imagine one rapid, six miles long, hurtling 1,200 cfs of whitewater through a tiny, rock-strewn gorge you've just pictured the Savage. In the entire run there are only one hundred yards of flat water. From put-in to take-out the paddler concentrates all his technical skill and reflexes in threading the needle through a jungle of rocks and holes. All this tight maneuvering is done within the confines of a narrow gorge (seldom more than fifty feet wide) that seems to be always twisting around a corner.

Another challenge of the Savage is its surprising swiftness. A good racer can cover the six miles in approximately half-an-hour. About a mile from the start, just below a broken dam, the river opens into the best spot for "playing." Swift, narrow tongues of water force you toward Memorial Rock and Triple Drop, the river's heaviest rapids. Aside from this area, used annually as a slalom course, there are few playing places. Eddies are small and hard to catch. Normally, there is only one narrow channel. Although a road runs from put-in to take-out, this slalom course is one of the few vantage points for the entire six miles, due to a separating layer of thick brush.

Since the river is controlled totally by a dam immediately above the put-in, it is wise to check the running schedule with local authorities. Many a paddler trying to squeeze in that third run of the day has found himself literally high and dry on a rock after the water was shut off like a faucet. A level of 600 to 1,500 cfs is optimum.

But when it's running, the Savage is a powerful, demanding river, challenging the boater every second he is on the water. There is little leisurely cruising, and the scenery from where the paddler kneels is less than impressive. But when the river spits you out into the lazy Potomac at the end, you feel the exhilaration of having mastered a difficult but delightful piece of whitewater.

Cheat River

CLASS: 4

DESCRIPTION: Broad riverbed littered with massive boulders, tight but powerful rapids of varying length.

STANDARD RUN: Put in at Albright, W.Va. (off Rte. 26); 11 mi. to Jenkinsburg Bridge.

LOCATION: 1 hr. S of Pittsburgh, Pa.; 3½ hrs. W of Washington, D.C.

RUNNING SEASON: March through mid-July, September through early November.

No boater likes to paddle where he can't see. The prospect of paddling down a blind chute into a labyrinth of house-size boulders, of being swept along at ten miles per hour scarcely able to see daylight, is about as attractive as running headlong into a pitchfork factory at midnight. Because of this prevalent and justifiable fear, the Cheat, until about five years ago, remained a run for the expert and the unwary. Today, an increase in both boating skills and the river's popularity has made it easy to find and follow some local Theseus through this Minoan maze.

From Albright the river starts out broad and shallow, but it soon squeezes into a canyon, tumbling over rocky ledges. For about a third of the way boaters are greeted by the towering Symphlegades of Big Nasty, a steeply pitched boulder garden that the boater must maneuver on blind faith. From this point, steep, rocky rapids come in quick succession. Mile-long boulder gardens are separated by brief, flat pools. In the major rapids large haystacks and tricky countercurrents keep the paddler constantly on his guard.

If threading this needle in your kayak still seems a bit far off, the paddler can experience much of the thrill and all of the beauty of this wilderness canyon on a commercial raft trip. Expert guides make a safe trip, and talking to them is an excellent way to learn about getting started in whitewater. However you view it, the Cheat is one of several West Virginia canyons that is too lovely and too much fun to miss.

C-1 SLALOM RACER

A C-1 (single-man canoe) slalom racer prepares to back his boat through a reverse gate. Even for the casual cruiser, racing is a good way to sharpen skills.

DONNA BERGLAND
World competition kayakist (opposite top) plays in a hole. Her boat is held in place by the curling pattern of the water sweeping back on itself.

KAYAK OR CANOE?
Boat designs look similar (opposite center) but you kneel in a C-1 (canoe) and use a single-bladed paddle, as opposed to sitting and using a double blade in a K-1 (kayak).

OHIOPYLE FALLS ON THE YOUGHIOGHENY
A herd of rafters (opposite bottom) paddle upstream from the put-in pool to take a closer look at the falls. Commercial outfitters run trips here from Memorial to Labor Day.

THE RAPIDS
A river guide in a kayak (below) helps rafters stay on the tongue.

Gauley River

CLASS: 5–6

DESCRIPTION: Smashingly powerful; short killer rapids separated by brief pools (thank God).

STANDARD RUN: Put in at Summersville Dam, W.Va.; 16 mi. to Peters Creek.

LOCATION: 5 hrs. SW of Washington, D.C.; 30 mi. E of Charleston, W.Va.

RUNNING SEASON: April through July, October and November—guaranteed water releases.

Most rivers above Class 2 are wrapped in a mantle of myth. Hair-raising rapids take on names, no one knows exactly how. Some commemorate a superstar's blunder (George's Rock), others are merely descriptive (Washing Machine). For eastern paddlers, the Gauley is a river that defies exaggeration.

Having mastered the Grand Canyon's Lava Falls is no sure ticket to surviving Iron Ring or Pure Screaming Hell. In spring nearly 3,000 cfs of current pound through the Gauley Gorge over ten-foot ledges and through incredibly steep boulder fields, all laced with yawning holes, just waiting to gobble up and spit out all but the experts.

At Sweet Falls the river caroms off the tight walls of the canyon, making a sharp S turn and then plunging over a ten-foot waterfall. John Sweet, a contemporary paddling legend, was the only one to run it in 1968, when the river was first explored.

At Iron Ring the whole river pours down a six-foot slide into a massive Class-6 hole. A boat-crunching left passage demands you leave this hole on the far right and upright. Swimming this one could spell disaster.

The Gauley is the bad dream of every paddler who is losing his nerve. If your equipment isn't O.K. or your roll isn't solid, stay home. But if you have that mixture of common sense and skill, you will find the Gauley River an experience never to be forgotten. And when someone talks of Table Rock, Lost Paddle, or Five Boat Hole, it will recall one of the toughest paddling challenges you've ever had.

New River

CLASS: 5

DESCRIPTION: Broad, large-volume river; heavy water; short, steep, staircase rapids.

STANDARD RUN: Put in at Thurmond, W.Va.; 14 mi. to Fayetteville Station.

LOCATION: 1 hr. E. of Charleston, W.Va.; 5 hrs. SW of Washington, D.C.

RUNNING SEASON: March through November.

Paddling through a broad, placid stretch in your kayak, the first three miles have offered nothing but the awesome vistas of the eight-hundred-foot New River Gorge. Suddenly your ears pick up an ominous thundering. Rounding a corner, you see the huge rapids everyone has told you about. The whole river drops over the edge out of sight. Aiming for what looks like the best slot, you find yourself instantly swept into a churning mass of white that is cascading steeply into the pool below.

For the remaining miles, the new River forms a staircase of short, dramatic rapids followed by brief pools of a few hundred yards. The rapids drop off steeply, forcing a large volume of water around several large rocks. Towering haystacks, huge keeper holes, and continuous heavy water present the main challenge. A prime example is Greyhound Bus Stop—a river-wide hole. As the water spills over a mammoth submerged rock, its sheer force makes the current curl back on itself. This curler just below the rock can catch and hold the unwary paddler, flipping him end over end in a dizzy and sometimes dangerous spin.

For the experienced Class-4 decked boat paddler, the New offers a good chance to move up to Class-5 heavy water. The current is powerful and tricky, but the short rapids and quiet pools make it a forgiving stream and an error will probably result in a bouncy swim, rather than a smashed boat or shoulder.

If all this sounds a little above your level, you can view the magnificent New River by commercial raft. A steep, thickly forested gorge towers above both sides of the river. Mountainous boulders line the shore, tortured into fantastic shapes by millennia of pounding river current. Its sheer size and remote beauty make it one of the most impressive rivers in the East.

Whether you run the New by raft, kayak, or C-1, you will experience the double thrill of heavy whitewater combined with majestic scenery.

SHIFTING WEIGHT
Rafters scramble to the upstream side (opposite) as they drop into the Yough's Double Hydraulic. This weight shift spreads the load and allows the raft to ride over the rapid without flipping.

LUGBILL AND HERN
These two world-class racers (right) tilt their *homemade, low-volume C-2 downstream as they peel out into the main current.*

SOUTHEAST

Though a relatively new whitewater territory compared to the Northeast and Mid-Atlantic regions, the Southeast has become a popular haven for all eastern paddlers. This is largely due to the growth of several permanent canoe training camps and to a well-earned reputation for lots of year-round, *warm*, heavy water.

River types vary extremely within this region, from the continuous, canyoned rivers of Alabama, to the slow, meandering streams in the south Georgia swamplands, to the ledgy, mountain runoff streams of the Tennessee Valley.

In the northern section of Tennessee and the Carolinas lies a true hotdogger's Mecca. The water and weather are warm. The long boulder fields of the Mid-Atlantic have yielded to steep, ledgy drops pouring into open, playable pools with classic hydraulics and trails of haystacks. These rivers strike a nice balance between the technical boulder-choked streams of the Northeast and the unimpeded, huge-volume sluices of the West. Here, paddling expertise calls for a blend of rock-dodging and heavy-water skills.

Another attraction of this region is the long running season. Most rivers can be run from early March right through November. Due to the TVA's dam releases or predictable summer rains, many maintain solid Class-3 and -4 levels through July and August.

Clubs in this region are extremely active and friendly to newcomers and outsiders. But often comradery can supercede common sense, and it is up to the individual paddler, not the trip leader, to avoid rivers beyond his ability.

The film *Deliverance* portrayed many of the rural Southeasterners in a terribly unkind, unrealistic light and resentment of paddlers is justifiably strong. Remember: It is your legal and moral responsibility to obtain the owner's permission both at put-ins and take-out's.

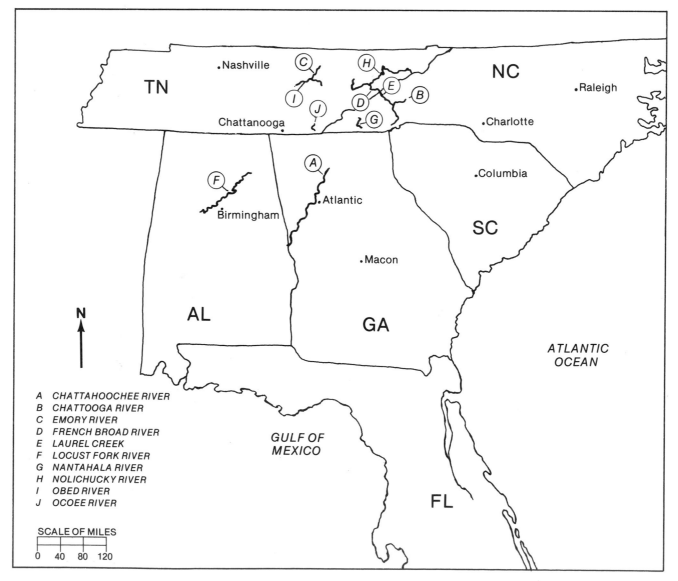

A   CHATTAHOOCHEE RIVER
B   CHATTOOGA RIVER
C   EMORY RIVER
D   FRENCH BROAD RIVER
E   LAUREL CREEK
F   LOCUST FORK RIVER
G   NANTAHALA RIVER
H   NOLICHUCKY RIVER
I   OBED RIVER
J   OCOEE RIVER

SCALE OF MILES
0   40   80   120

NANTAHALA RIVER
The Nantahala Falls (opposite) is one of the most popular rapids in the Southeast. This paddler proves that open boats can handle heavy water, if the boater is experienced.

Ocoee River

CLASS: 3–5

DESCRIPTION: Medium width; continuous, very fast, big open water; few boulders, many ledges.

STANDARD RUN: Put in below #2 Dam (wooden) just off Rte. 64, 5 mi. W of Ducktown, Tenn.; 5 mi. to take-out at #2 Power Station, (this is the only run possible on the Ocoee).

LOCATION: 55 mi. E of Chattanooga, Tenn.; 5 mi. W of Ducktown, Tenn.; near Tenn./N.C. border.

RUNNING SEASON: All year round from 10 A.M. to 6 P.M. until 1980, depending on dam releases.

The Ocoee is a born-again river. For thirty-five years it remained buried under a flume and carved up by three TVA dams to meet state power needs. Now a dam has burst and the Ocoee flows again—for at least three years. The river's #2 Power Station and its wooden dam and flume are temporarily closed for repairs, and authorities are releasing water from Dam #3 over the original river bed.

For most of its five miles the river is an open, continuous sluice with the current shunted this way and that by low ledges coming out from the bank. It is not a technical river—boulders and sharp bends are few. But the water is big and the haystacks are high. Commercial rafters normally use fourteen-footers (a K-1 is approximately thirteen feet) because the twelve-footers easily flip in the large, abundant holes.

Considering the magnitude of the water, the Ocoee is a forgiving river.

Most holes wash out; keepers are relatively few. There is very little chance of pinning yourself or your boat. Route 64 follows along the entire run and cars can be spotted easily. Normally, the five miles go by very swiftly and most paddlers can fit in two runs in one day. Nonetheless, this river has its dangers and is not to be attempted by less experienced intermediates just seeking a bouncy sluice. Many rapids are Class 5 and continuous. Eddies are sparse, and dumping means at least a half-mile swim. The Ocoee is also a tricky river to read. It flows over a bed that has been dry for more than three decades, so wave patterns are irregular and loaded with cross currents.

If you have the skill, run it now but don't count on the Ocoee for your children. Officials say the repairs should be completed by spring 1980, and the Ocoee will again go underground. Currently, schedules release water at 10 A.M. and slam the sluice gates shut at 6 P.M. (Many a paddler has been literally left high and dry.) The Ocoee is beautiful and exciting, and it is unfortunate that its life span will be so short. But perhaps this river can awaken all of us to the great number of whitewater streams already lost and the effort we must exert to save the remaining few.

CHATOOGA RIVER
Peeling out of an eddy takes surprising teamwork, as does any maneuver in a C-2. The bowman draws the boat out into the main current, while his sternman powers forward to augment the turning stroke.

Nolichucky River

CLASS: 3–4+

DESCRIPTION: Large-volume, technical river with steep cascades; long rock gardens; many submerged boulders; several flat stretches.

STANDARD RUN: Put in at Poplar, N.C.; 11½ mi. to Erwin, Tenn.

LOCATION: 1½ hrs. E of Knoxville, Tenn. River crosses N.C.–Tenn. border.

RUNNING SEASON: March through late October (late summer runs can be thin); occasional midwinter runs possible for the hardy.

"Rafters? Inconsiderate, every one of 'em." Many experienced canoeists and kayakers regard all raft paddlers as dangerously inept, lacking any river courtesy, and not having earned the right to enjoy whitewater. This prejudice is not totally justified— but many are the kayakers who have been slammed into rock walls by a raft loaded with jolly, unaware "paddlers."

Despite the "Hard-boaters" snarls, a raft can provide the would-be kayaker with a marvelous starting point and the appreciative outdoorsman a view of nature at her most dramatic. The broad, powerful waters of the Nolichucky, made popular by commerical rafters, flow through one of the Southeast's deeper, more majestic canyons. Craggy, sheer granite cliffs rise up 2,000 feet from the water's edge, alternately bare and covered with clinging hardwoods. Jumbles of water-etched, house-size boulders crowd the river's edge. At several spots along the gorge wall, waterfalls cascade into the main river. In midwinter these falls completely freeze, rewarding the chilled cruiser with magnificent natural ice sculptures.

The Nolichucky is a large-volume river. Long fields of broad table rocks split the river into many channels, creating a maze of currents and countercurrents. Long Rapids winds and twists through a half-mile of these large boulders and, while the current is relatively slow, it cannot be mastered by muscle alone. The Rock Rapids have proved the river's power to many a boater with slow reflexes who pried too late, broached, and ended up literally high and dry on the rocks.

The Nolichucky is most powerful at the beginning and then tapers off. The initial rapids, such as Sousehole and On the Rock, become Class 4+ in high water. After leaving the canyon, three miles from take-out, the river, now shallower, becomes Class 2. It is possible to make a shorter run to eliminate the final, slower section by taking out on some of the local roads south of Erwin.

RAFTERS
Commercial rafts are common sights on most of the large, popular rivers of the Southeast. Unlike many of the Western tours, here passengers are expected to pull their own weight.

Laurel Creek into French Broad River

CLASS: *Laurel Creek—4. French Broad—2-4*
DESCRIPTION: *Laurel Creek*—Steep, rock-strewn gorge; swift continuous current with many vertical drops. *French Broad*—Wide with long, open rock gardens and some big vertical drops; with strong current.
STANDARD RUN: Put in at Rte. 209 bridge, 6 mi. S of Hot Springs, N.C.; 5½ mi. to Laurel Creek–French Broad confluence; 4 mi. to Hot Springs, N.C. (single-day trip).
LOCATION: 3½ hrs. NW of Charlotte, N.C.; 1 hr. N of Asheville, N.C.; 1¼ hrs. E of Knoxville, Tenn.; near Tenn.-N.C. border.
RUNNING SEASON: Possible February through October; suggested May and June.

They say that in the East you don't remember the river, you remember the rocks. Certainly the rocks give any river its character. Jumble them too closely together, and paddling becomes more nerve-racking than it is worth. Make them too scarce and the stream loses its excitement. Most boaters spend their time seeking a river with just the right balance.

Laurel Creek is one stream that offers the right balance, with a natural slalom course and the perfect blend of rock dodging and open river. It warms up moving through two miles of easily negotiated rock gardens. Then with surprising swiftness, the river tumbles down a steep rock-strewn gorge. For three continuous miles the boater frantically draws and pries as a constant current pushes him through a tight mass of table-size boulders. Sudsy Hole is one of several nearly vertical cascades that drop six to seven feet into a riverwide roller. These holes can be real keepers at higher water levels. At Triple Drop the river narrows to one-third its normal width and plunges over three three-foot ledges in less than twenty feet, demanding some real zigzagging.

Working the final three miles of Laurel Creek is pure delight for the Class-4 paddler who is up to the challenge. You bite off as much river as your arms and nerves can stand, then swing into a side eddy, exhale, and slump your shoulders for a second before moving out into the current again.

After five and a half miles Laurel Creek spits the boater out onto the French Broad where he enjoys the last four miles of the exciting Ashton–to–Hot Springs run. This wide murky stream flows over a smooth rock bed creating a long series of high standing waves. In heavy water it is an open, bouncy sleigh ride broken by a few surprisingly tricky and demanding ledges. Frank Bell Rapids, named after an expert cruiser who ran the French Broad from its source all the way to the Gulf of Mexico, is a triple-drop ledge with a mass of countercurrents. Here, the three drops are very steep and end in a river-wide hole and boiler that can toss your boat in any direction.

The French Broad River can be paddled from its headwaters all the way to the Gulf with several popular runs in the 125 miles between Rosman, North Carolina, and Newport, Tennessee, presenting challenges from Class 1 to Class 6. One of the best learners' runs is from Rosman to Brevard. The river is slow and takes some muscle, but the short rock gardens and chutes give the novice a good sense of current and also give him a chance to practice for the greater challenges downstream.

NANTAHALA RIVER
Playing a hole is usually considered a privilege of decked boats. But, with the right skill and balance, open boaters can hold themselves broadside to a curling hydraulic.

NANTAHALA RIVER
Many believe that racing an open boat solo (above left) is "too much" for a woman. This girl proves it's not so in the 1977 Nationals.
Rafters (above right) are temporarily submerged in a hole and struggle to pull themselves out.

BOWMAN ON THE SHIP OF STATE
(below) In or out of the Oval Office, a president is only as good as his advisors. Here on the Chatooga, Jimmy Carter entrusts himself to a guide without a life jacket.

Obed and Emory Rivers

CLASS: *Obed*—3–4. *Emory*—2

DESCRIPTION: *Obed*—Narrow and winding, rocky stream with riffles and cascades separated by still pools. *Emory*—Narrow and rocky; slow but continuous current; many ledges and chutes followed by moving pools.

STANDARD RUN: Put in on Daddy's Creek, Tenn. (via local road off Rte. 62); 11 mi. to Nemo, Tenn. (past confluence with Emory River), 8 mi. more on Emory into Oakdale, Tenn.

LOCATION: 45 min. NW of Oak Ridge, Tenn.

RUNNING SEASON: March through late May, September through November; summer runs often possible due to heavy rains.

The Obed and Emory are part of the large network of relatively small streams flowing off the southern tip of the broad Cumberland Plateau into the East Tennessee Valley. Within an hour's drive of this area run the Clear Fork, Clear Creek (into the Obed), the Caney Fork, Little Tennessee, upper Daddy's Creek, and some beautiful stretches of the upper Obed. The Hiwassee and Nolichucky are just a little farther away. All these streams offer Knoxville and Oak Ridge paddlers a convenient smorgasbord of small-to-medium-size streams from Class 1 to Class 6.

The intermediate run begins with the final two miles of Daddy's Creek running north to the **Obed.** Putting in at the Devil's Breakfast Table, a massive natural rock sculpture with a broad rock table perched high above the creek, the boater twists his way through a series of little drops and pools. These rapids are short and intricate, but the lack of volume makes them Class 2. At the entrance to the Obed, speed, volume, and difficulty increase. Most of the rapids have a series of "lead-in riffles" before a steep, usually open cascade, followed by a flat pool at the bottom. Rock Garden is a solid Class-4 hazard that should be scouted or portaged by the intermediate. The river plunges over a staircase of three off-angle cascades, demanding some sharp wriggling to line up for each chute.

A steep rock canyon follows the Obed during this entire run toward the Tennessee Valley. Several river-level caves offer fascinating little labyrinths, which you can paddle into at the right water level. In the final third of the run Clear Creek enters from the north, adding substantial volume and creating a long series of unobstructed standing waves in several downstream sections. A half-mile from the take-out, the Obed mingles its surprisingly clear waters with the muddy Emory and flows southeast to the town of Nemo.

The **Emory** is a popular learner's river which many paddlers prefer to run on Saturday as a warm-up for the more challenging Obed, which is upstream. Although putting in at Nemo, the boater·is immediately confronted with the river's toughest rapid. Nemo Rapid is a steep Class-3 cascade with two mid-current rocks that enjoy broaching open boats. This short stretch is easily portaged by the beginner, and the rest of the run is seldom above Class 2. A swift, continuous current flows over easily negotiated ledges and long rock-free chutes. The major difficulty is lining up at the top of the drop. There is plenty of water that is always moving fairly swiftly, even between rapids. Frequently open boaters have to backpaddle through high standing waves. In the final two miles before the Oakdale take-out, the river suddenly broadens, and the steady flow slows to almost a standstill.

The river may have once been as clear as the Obed, but strip mining upstream has choked the waters with a sand-colored silt. However, it is still a scenic trip. The river passes through rolling hills covered with oak, maple, and poplar, and the bank occasionally rises to a two-hundred-foot bluff. If you are a beginner with a friend who has a taste for Class 4 to 5, send him on Saturday to the upper Obed or Daddy's Creek while you run the Emory. Then you can both run the lower Obed on Sunday.

OBED RIVER

(opposite) *Just because the rocks don't break the surface doesn't mean they aren't there. It's the ones you can't see that always crunch you.*

THE ENDER, ETC.

When running the river is simply not enough (left), you might try an ender. Plough your bow into the right shaped hole and flip end-over-end. Your balance had better be exquisite and your roll perfect. Otherwise, just cruising over the falls (below) will give you all the tilt and terror you need.

Nantahala River

CLASS: 3

DESCRIPTION: Swift continuous current; constant haystacks and low drops; many holes, few keepers.

STANDARD RUN: Put in below power plant on Rte. 19 above Nantahala N.C.; 8 mi. to take-out at Wesser Falls, near Nantahala Outdoor Center.

LOCATION: 4 hrs. SW of Winston-Salem, N.C.; 13 mi. S of Bryson City, N.C.

RUNNING SEASON: All year, depending on TVA water releases.

This river has recently become the focal point of whitewater boating in the East. Paddlers who have scarcely seen a sousehole south of Boston make thousand-mile pilgrimages to North Carolina's whitewater Mecca—the Nantahala River. The main reason hordes of experts, intermediates, and rank beginners flock to this eight-mile stretch of Class-3 water is the Nantahala Outdoor Center, a year-round canoe and kayak training camp designed for all levels of paddlers. Many camps teach whitewater boating, but very few give instruction as expertly or thoroughly as the Center. At the end of a week's concentrated training, many a total novice has gained enough ability and confidence to handle and even play the river's Class-3 rapids.

The Nantahala is the best training river in the South. It has a continuous flow with few pools and an even gradient; it drops approximately thirty-three feet per mile. A good distribution of chair- to table-size rocks in a 600-cfs current provides constant, safe playing spots from Class 1 to 3. These are the kind of holes you can easily drop into, spin your paddle, and even do some enders; and you can get out of them just as easily.

The atmosphere of the camp and the size of the rapids invite you to play and experiment with new maneuvers. You may watch the expert instructors or racers in training and decide that a certain hole is not really so tough after all. Since everyone is trying his utmost to improve, there are a lot of wipe-outs. But the penalties for error are not threatening, and you are seldom tested beyond your ability.

Nantahala Falls and Wesser Falls are the major exceptions to this rule. The former is a Class-5 rapid located right below the slalom course and take-out at the outdoor center. It is a two-step drop that demands a very fast zigzag. Wesser, virtually unrunnable, lies immediately downstream and has been survived by a few experts who consider themselves very lucky.

Whether you are a novice dedicated to gaining the most expertise in the shortest possible time or an expert who wants to train in an atmosphere of camaraderie and information swapping, the Nantahala is an ideal whitewater river.

NANTAHALA NATIONALS
Contestants compete in the 1977 National Open Canoe Whitewater Championships. (left) *The bowman lines up for the next gate while the stern paddler pries her end away from the gate at hand.* (below) *Paddlers try to duck under the same slalom pole, with disastrous results.*

UPPER OBED RIVER
Open boaters who plunge over steep drops have the extra worry of taking on a boatful of water. (opposite) *This homemade partial deck offers a partial solution.*

Chattooga River

CLASS: 3 + –5

DESCRIPTION: Medium width, rocky; many ledges and short, flat pools; heavy, swift current.

STANDARD RUN: Put in at Earls Ford (via dirt road on Ga. side of river); 15 mi. to Rte. 76 bridge (section III run); 7½ mi. more to Lake Tugaloo; landing on S.C. side of lake backwater for take-out (section IV run).

LOCATION: 3 hrs. NE of Atlanta, Ga., in Cherokee, Chattahoochee, and Sumter Natl. Forests. River forms NW boundary between Ga. and S.C.

RUNNING SEASON: Suggested March through October; optimum gauge 1.5–2 ft.

"Awesome, overpowering, spectacular!" Such rave reviews are usually reserved for huge-volume western rivers with larger-than-life haystacks surging through broad, towering canyons. Easterners rarely think of their region's rivers in these terms. But the Chattooga deserves all these superlatives and more, both for its rapids and unequaled scenery.

This winding, medium-width river boasts over twenty-five Class-3-to-5 rapids in the twenty-three miles of Sections III and IV. Huge truck-size boulders create tight twisty channels and vertical ledges with narrow, hard-to-find slots that require exceptional maneuvering and water reading. But the Chattooga holds more than technical challenges. Diagonal tongues, caused by water flowing over large, flat boulders assault the paddler weaving through a boulder patch. River-wide hydraulics lurk beneath several of the sheer falls with enough power to undo even the strongest boaters.

The Chattooga is a dangerous river that claims boaters' lives every year. Many are unnecessary victims of the "Deliverance syndrome": Totally inexperienced boaters and rafters rushing to the Chattooga, location of the movie Deliverance, boasting, "If Burt Reynolds can do it, so can I." (Actually, the toughest running was done by Payson Kennedy and two other expert paddlers, with many years of experience behind them.) But this uncalculated insanity is not the only cause of Chattooga tragedy. It is a river that demands scouting. So many of the rapids cannot be run by less than expert paddlers. Each paddler must rely on his common sense and not his bravado in deciding what to portage.

Painted Rock, in Section III, an uneven ledge of large boulders followed by a foaming rock garden and a massive boulder literally painted with aluminum, is often portaged by open boaters. Bull Sluice, a horseshoe-shaped fall dropping ten feet in two steps, demands a tight, narrow zigzag and should be portaged by all but the top experts.

Section IV holds some of the most thrilling whitewater in the entire Southeast. A little less than halfway along, Woodall Shoals presents a portage for virtually all paddlers. Corkscrew, Jawbone, and Sockemdog are constricted ledge drops with an enormous volume that many experts have portaged in high water.

The Chattooga flows through a wilderness choked with life. Lush beds of rhododendron and mountain laurel, broken only by an occasional massive boulder, border crystal-clear side eddies stocked with brook trout. Deep woods of pine and spruce climb up rugged canyon walls, alternating with hardwood forests on the lower banks. This is a river where the paddler is more likely to glimpse a deer, hawk, or even an eagle than he is another human being.

The Chattooga exemplifies the rich, fertile beauty of the wooded East combined with a maximum whitewater challenge. It should not be attempted by anyone without an experienced mentor who knows the river, but it should also not be missed by any capable paddler who can make the trip.

Note: Paddler registration is required at all put-in spots.

Chattahoochee River

CLASS: 2
DESCRIPTION: Narrow, twisty, very rocky; many shoals and long rock gardens; short, moving pools.
STANDARD RUN: Put in at old mill 3½ mi. S of Helen, Ga.; 14 mi. to Duncan Bridge, just upstream of Lake Lanier.
LOCATION: 85 mi. NE of Atlanta, Ga., in Chattahoochee Natl. Forest.
RUNNING SEASON: Possible year round; summer levels often thin. Suggested March to June and September to November.

A river tamed has lost its drama. Its waters, pent up by a concrete dam, are released in cautious, measured amounts, flowing the same every day all year long. And like a man trapped in a large city, it cuts a comfortable channel, pushing steadily throughout its entire length.

But for a wild river, like the upper Chattahoochee, change is the only routine. Depending upon immediate rain and seasonal runoff, it swells to torrential flood, then suddenly drops to a thin trickle. This ever-changing energy tumbles rocks of all sizes together, creating everything from shallow riffles over pebbly shoals to deep narrow channels through head-high boulders. For the whitewater student, this makes a challenge of infinite variety and surprise.

It is this variety that makes the Chattahoochee an excellent place to discover whitewater. Seldom widening to more than fifty feet, this narrow, rocky stream flows alternately over long shoals; hundred-yard boulder gardens; short, straight flumes; and staircase ledges. Having a Class-1+-to-2+ level, it forces the beginner to read all types of water and make fast, definite decisions.

Most of the rapids are tight and technical. On Buck Shoals the paddler picks his way through a quarter-mile of rock garden, then suddenly slides down through an eight-foot-wide S-turning channel into Canoe-Eating Rock, an undercut boulder that splits the channel in half. Three Ledges winds around a twenty-foot boulder, making three small vertical drops in quick succession, demanding that the novice zigzag powerfully across the current. If all this sounds terrifying, do not get frightened. It is scarcely ever above a Class-2+ challenge, and frequent pools make ideal rest and recovery spots.

Locust Fork River

CLASS: 4–5 (closed boat)
DESCRIPTION: Medium width; continuous and steep; huge boulders, large keeper holes; winding and fast.
STANDARD RUN: Put in at end of chairlift outside Ft. Payne, Ala.; 8 mi. to take-out in Canyon Land Park.
LOCATION: 2 hrs. NE of Birmingham, Ala., on Rte. 59 (near Ga. border).
RUNNING SEASON: January through late March.

Take a look at the first rapid. If you have to think, you should not put in. From the moment you drive through the first haystack until you swing into the take-out eddy eight miles later, you are trapped in the deepest canyon east of the Mississippi. Deciding halfway along that this is not your kind of water will not alter a thing.

For this reason, the Locust Fork should be run by experts only. Though most of the rapids are only Class 3+ with Class-5 sections that can be portaged, it is nevertheless a dangerous river. The limestone green water races through the canyon dropping steadily and creating continuous rapids with huge standing waves. An Idaho boater would feel at home in this deep canyon with its western style water. But an endless jumble of large boulders forming tight technical rock gardens should remind you that you are still facing the eastern challenge of instant maneuvering. Often these house-size boulders split the current into several tight channels with ninety-degree turns that must be read blind. Swift "cushions" of water flow around the rocks, dumping the unwary into frothing holes with enough power to recycle him for a week. With sparse eddies and few letups the Locust Fork demands total concentration.

But if you do manage to grab one of the rare side eddies, pause a minute and study a canyon as awesome as the river itself. Chalky limestone cliffs, with endless, wavy striations, tower nearly 2,000 feet above the light green water. Sparrow hawks and an occasional golden eagle can be spotted gliding on an updraft in lazy spirals. For a view from a different perspective, you can hike the Canyon Park trail that follows the rim of this vertical gorge. Whether viewed from above or below, the Locust Fork Canyon is one of the most magnificent sights in the Southeast and should not be missed.

A warning: A twelve-foot vertical fall approximately four miles downstream from the put-in demands that every group have at least one guide familiar with the river. In addition, water level should not exceed the height of the stone dock at the put-in.

SUNLIGHT AND SPARKLING WATERS
So beautiful on a quiet lake, these can cause a blinding glare in rapids and make water-reading nearly impossible.

HIGH WATER, LOW WATER
River level is everything in white water. The kayakist playing in the riverwide hydraulic (opposite top) and the open boaters splashing through the curler (opposite bottom) are in roughly the same spot on the same rapids.

WILL HE OR WON'T HE?
An open boater on the Nantahala (below) stabs the foam and draws for dear life while anxious kayakists prepare to rescue.

SOUTH CENTRAL

The South Central is actually two regions, the Ozarks and Texas, linked more by style of paddling than geography. Most paddling is done in open boats on long rivers for either weekend or week-long "float trips." Kayaks are rare, as is truly heavy, decked-boat-only water. And both sections offer whitewater campers a variety of forgiving, and often remote, rivers.

The rolling, hilly Ozarks, centering around the Arkansas-Missouri border, boast a network of popular spring-fed streams. River gradients are not overly steep, and large rocks are rare. Seldom do paddlers encounter a rapid above Class 3 or a river continuously above Class 2. Typically, rapids consist of constricted banks, shoaly gravel bars, and overhanging trees. Flash floods frequently raise river levels as much as thirty feet overnight, causing swift currents and the dangerous challenge of weaving through a maze of trees.

The popular paddling season runs from March to November, but huge underground springs feed many of the region's rivers, making the season more a matter of personal comfort than water level.

In Texas, water of any kind is hard to come by. But the few whitewater streams available offer hundreds of miles of paddling, with the remote canyons of the Rio Grande providing the majority. Several streams fed by reservoirs or underground springs maintain a constant flow year round. But the most exciting rivers are the least dependable—along the Edward Plateau autumn rain storms cause flash flooding. Texas clubs have developed a network of spotters who quickly pass the word when the water's up. September and October constitute the prime season, with the lowest water levels in spring. Except for the Rio Grande, the water is similar to that of the Ozarks: Long flat stretches of varying speed alternate with shoaly rapids and constricted S-turns.

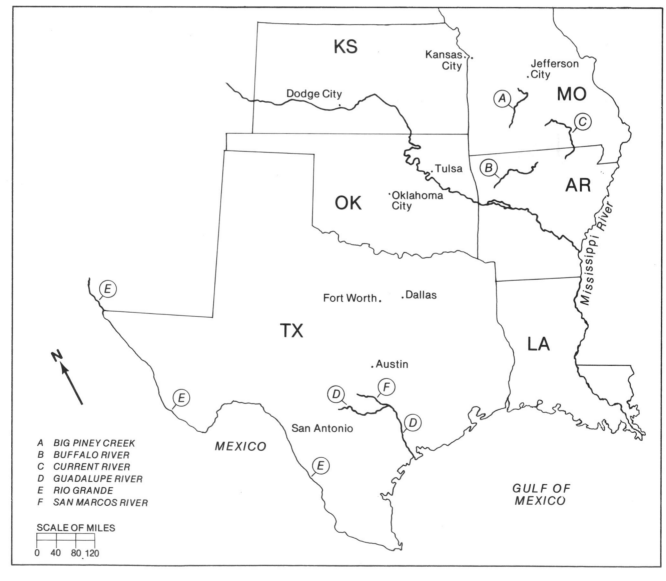

A BIG PINEY CREEK
B BUFFALO RIVER
C CURRENT RIVER
D GUADALUPE RIVER
E RIO GRANDE
F SAN MARCOS RIVER

SCALE OF MILES

0   40   80 120

RIO GRANDE
The joy of paddling (opposite) is not always appreciated by younger passengers. Perhaps she is crying for her father who unwisely left his lifejacket behind.

GUADALUPE RIVER
An all-too-familiar sight in Texas (above): the barechested whitewater paddler. The Chute Rapids seen here are forgiving, and the boaters capable. But any white water requires a lifejacket. The law demands that you carry it and common sense demands you wear it. These canoeists (center) running a drop in the Rio Grande, have lashed their life vests to the thwarts, making them totally worthless if the boat dumps.

RIO GRANDE
Polar bear paddlers (opposite top) start out on a New Year's Day trip. In Texas and the Ozarks the rivers run all year around, and so do the paddlers.

PECOS RIVER
With a boatful of gear, canoe campers (opposite) negotiate a rock-strewn drop.

Rio Grande—The Upper Canyons

CLASS: 2–3

DESCRIPTION: Broad and shallow; some small rock gardens and shoals alternate with house-size boulder patches; much flat.

STANDARD RUN: Put in at Lajitas, Tex.; 17 mi. through Santa Elena Canyon (1–1½ days), 40 mi. of flat (2–4 days) to O'Rally Ranch (Mariscal put-in), 7 mi. through Mariscal Canyon to Solis take-out. Boquillas Canyon put-in at Rio Grande Village; 28 mi. to take-out at Stillwell's Crossing (1–2 days).

LOCATION: Western tip of Big Bend Natl. Park, SW corner of Tex., many miles from anywhere.

RUNNING SEASON: Possible all year round, depending on water level. Best time is September and October. Lowest in spring.

Most paddlers believe you have to be a hairy-chested expert to view a magnificent canyon from your own boat. But the Santa Elena, considered one of America's three most scenic canyons, makes an awesomely beautiful exception. Dark, polished limestone cliffs tower seventeen hundred feet above the water, leaving only a narrow slit of blue sky overhead.

After the Lajitas put-in the Rio Grande flows through Colorado Canyon, which contains short series of rock gardens, demanding technical maneuvering. Then, after paddling through several miles of vast open desert, you enter Santa Elena Canyon.

Gravel bars constrict the flow, creating shoaly rapids with playful, bouncy standing waves. You're sure this mild sleigh ride will go on forever until you turn the corner and face the legendary Rockslide Rapids. Millennia ago, a massive rockslide dumped thousands of house-size boulders from the Mexican side into the river.

Rockslide is a dangerous rapid. The current appears calm, normally Class 2, but an incredibly swift current can sweep you through an ever-narrowing rocky maze into a one-foot-wide channel. In the first two hundred yards, the river makes six S turns. Whirlpools develop that you just can't see. Basically it is a Class-2 run, but it is nearly impossible to scout and very difficult to read blind. If you dump, survival has nothing to do with swimming skill; 90 percent of the channels flow beneath undercut rocks. Portage this one unless you have a competent local guide.

After Santa Elena comes forty flat miles through the Coahuila Desert. It is a beautiful open vista with distant mountains rimming either horizon. Mariscal Canyon follows this stretch of desert. For seven miles the Rio Grande flows eighteen hundred feet beneath the canyon rim. Deep limestone caves, roofs forested with stalactites, and sculptured stone pillars make this a magnificent single-day paddle. Most of the rapids consist of constricted tricky turns, alternating with flat. Two small boulder patches call for Class-2 technical maneuvering.

Boquillas Canyon forms the final twenty-eight miles of the Rio Grande in Big Bend National Park. Boquillas slices through the Sierra del Carmen mountain range, creating a step canyon that staircases back 4600 feet from river to rim. If you have something to prove, you can chug the whole twenty-eight miles in a single day. But if you have any feeling for scenery at all, camp overnight and appreciate the wild horses and burros that graze along the terraces and the massive, richly colored, vertical walls.

Note: The Big Bend section of the Rio Grande is a Remote Area. Law and common sense require you to get a paddling and driving permit from one of the ranger stations. These no-limit permits register your presence with park rangers and inform you of paddling and driving conditions.

Rio Grande—The Lower Canyons

CLASS: 1+ –3+

DESCRIPTION: Broad flat mixed with short, steep boulder gardens; many sluices on turns.

STANDARD RUN: Put in at Stillwell's Crossing, Tex.; 90 mi. (approximately) to take out at cable crossing in Aqua Verde, 20 mi. S of Dryden, Tex. (sugg. 5 days, 4 nights).

LOCATION: Eastern corner of Big Bend Natl. Park, SW corner of Tex., many miles from anywhere

RUNNING SEASON: Possible all year round, depending on water level. Best time is September and October. Lowest in Spring.

Until 1968 fewer than sixty people had run the one hundred miles between Stillwell's Crossing and Dryden, Texas. Today the total is still under twelve hundred. If you want to be one of the few, you should have not only your paddling skills in order but also a solid knowledge of camping and first aid as well as a familiarity with the desert. This is a land where "civilization" consists of a border-patrol plane flying by once a month. Most city-dwelling paddlers find it difficult to conceive of a land so remote—or so beautiful.

Outlaw Flats, a vast, open vega area with high cliffs a mile and a half from the river edge, runs for the first thirty miles. A century ago, it was a haven for outlaws hiding out from Texas Rangers and Mexican Federales. Little has changed, and today narcotics smugglers make their homes in the caves dug out of the cliffs. Normally, these men have no great interest in paddlers, and campfire smoke will be their only signs. Horse, Boreland, and a few other short canyons break up this open tract with thousand-foot vertical cliffs and constricted S-turn rapids with swift, rock-free standing waves.

For the final sixty miles, Reagan Canyon runs virtually uninterrupted to the take-out at Dryden. The sheer height of the canyon will overwhelm the paddler just coming in from the open desert. The cliff walls rise sixteen hundred feet to the first terrace and up to thirty-five hundred feet to the next. Fortunately, this height varies and the canyon is wide, which keeps you from feeling that you are paddling in a sixty-mile tunnel.

At normal September levels, the water flows swiftly, making Class-1+ -to-2 relatively rock-free sleigh rides. Narrowing at the turns, surprisingly long tongues of current carry the boater past a beautiful panorama of sculptured rock. Three major Class-4 rapids lurk within this canyon and force the paddler to be wary and do more than just bounce through the waves. Hot Springs is a vertical eight-foot drop with chair-size boulders to dodge above and below. Camping here will allow you to take advantage of the natural hot springs feeding this 150-yard rapid.

Burro Bluff Rapid (Upper Madison Falls) is a jumble of huge boulders that demands Class-3+ maneuvering and can be scouted from above or run blind. Horseshoe Rapids (Lower Madison) is a steep six-foot drop in thirty yards, where high standing waves weave between house-size boulders.

Though the colors of rock strata are less dramatic than in the Grand Canyon, the variety of rock sculpture is every bit as awesome. This natural beauty, combined with the remote wilderness aura of the region, make the Rio Grande one of the unique, exquisite experiences possible only by canoe.

Warning: Rescue from this section of the Rio Grande is more difficult and less likely than anywhere in the United States. Large ranches (two hundred thousand acres) are sparsely manned and offer little hope. In case of injury, be prepared to carry your own party out. There have been occasional incidents between bandit-smugglers and paddlers, always with small parties. Always travel with a party of at least six people.

Indian artifacts can be found in many caves. Please leave them for all to enjoy.

RIO GRANDE

Desert mountains (opposite) *loom dark against a Texas sky. Here, in Colorado Canyon, the river broadens but still retains several open, interesting rapids.*

(below) *Hitting the slot. Sleek, low-gunwaled marathon boats such as this are ideal for fast cruising on the long, not-too-heavy rivers of the Southwest.*

Guadalupe River

CLASS: 3+

DESCRIPTION: Narrow and winding; swift current; many S turns; some steep drops; long stretches of flat water.

STANDARD RUN: Put in at Canyon Lake, Tex., just below dam; 10 mi. to bridge take-out in New Braunfels.

LOCATION: ½ hr. N of San Antonio, Tex.

RUNNING SEASON: All year round, totally dependent on dam releases and flash floods.

Texas whitewater is some of the least dependable in the country. Flash floods and indiscriminate reservoir releases are scarcely a foundation on which to build a paddling season, especially considering the vast distances most Lone Star boaters must travel to a put-in. The Guadalupe remains a delightfully convenient exception. Although it depends on Canyon Lake water for much of its volume, the releases are fairly constant all year round. If you live in San Antonio, you can make this ten-mile run any evening after work.

On release, a swift current of only 400 to 900 cfs sweeps over a narrow, winding riverbed of sharp S turns, making large, bouncy haystacks. Much of this run is open, with short flumes that spit you out into a placid but slowly moving pool. These open chutes alternate with fast, technical rock gardens with table-size boulders and Class-3 holes that have claimed many a boater who thought the Guadalupe was just a sleigh ride.

Horseshoe Falls represents a major danger point with a kitchen-size sousehole below a four-foot vertical drop. It is a Class-4 keeper and is generally treated too lightly by local paddlers. There is another hazard on the Guadalupe. On a hot summer Saturday canoes, kayaks, rafts, old innertubes, air-inflated waterbeds—just about anything that floats—will be launched into the stream by careless, unprepared hordes seeking a cool and exciting run into New Braunfels. Normally, everyone jostles downstream in a spirit of cooperation. But most of these floaters have no control, and it is up to you as a paddler to prevent tragedy.

This short section of the Guadalupe winds through a beautifully thick forest of oak, cedar, and cypress. The unusually lush Texas forest is part of the Edwards Plateau, through which roam most of the state's three million deer, often within site of the paddler or day hiker. For the local boater, the Guadalupe offers a convenient alternative if flash floods are not filling up another stream or if the Rio is just too far away. For the nomad paddler who is just passing through, the river offers an exceptional challenge in some of the lushest country in Texas.

San Marcos River

CLASS: Beginner–1+

DESCRIPTION: Narrow, winding, open stream; few obstacles; often shallow; continuous.

STANDARD RUN: Put in below spring in town of San Marcos, Tex.; 10½ mi. to Martindale Dam, 40 mi. more to confluence with Guadalupe (campsite).

LOCATION: 45 min. NW of San Antonio, Tex., in town of San Marcos.

RUNNING SEASON: All year round.

Rising out of the vast deserts of southern Texas near Del Rio, the high Edwards Plateau creates a several-hundred-foot-high escarpment running northeast toward Austin. At the base of these sandstone cliffs lies the Balcones Fault, a geological fracture from which hundreds of underground springs gush to the surface. It is from some of these great crystal-clear springs that the Frio, Medina, Pedernales, San Marcos, and countless other small streams claim their source.

The San Marcos Spring is probably the largest in the Fault. Each year it pumps millions of gallons down the river channel, fifty miles to its confluence with the Guadalupe. (For aesthetics' sake, the boater will want to put in below the town. San Marcos has built an amusement park around the spring, and the odds of hitting a glass-bottomed tourist boat are excellent.) The stream flows slowly but continuously, running clear and refreshingly cold under the hot Texas sun.

For the paddler who simply wants to paddle in current, the San Marcos is a great starting point. Outfitters in the town and at several other points along the river supply all equipment, including life jackets. The challenge of the water is very mild. The river twists often and the banks constrict, making some swift, open sluices. Frequently, pebbly shoals and small rock gardens demand some basic maneuvering. But the only real dangers are the downed trees lurking on the outside of a bend and an occasional small dam.

The irrigating waters of the San Marcos run through tree-lined banks and grassy farmlands. It is a scenic run and well worth a two- or three-day canoe and camping trip. Most of the surrounding land is privately owned and requires permission for camping, but ranchers are traditionally cooperative. Although far from Texas's greatest whitewater challenge, the San Marcos is always ready at the right water level whenever you want to paddle. This is no mean claim for a Lone Star river!

GUADALUPE RIVER

(right) *There are a few surprises on even the most familiar streams. One wrong move can put the paddler without a life jacket in peril.* (below) *One of Texas's most challenging rivers, the Guadalupe can be run all year round due to a combination of dam releases and flash floods.*

Big Piney Creek

CLASS: 1–3

DESCRIPTION: Narrow, winding, shallows; shoals and rock gardens; some swift sluices; long flat stretches.

STANDARD RUN: Put in on Indian Creek at Fort Douglas or at Phillips Ford, Ark., on Big Piney, just downstream of Fort Douglas; 17 mi. to take-out at Long Pool recreation area.

LOCATION: 2½ hrs. NW of Little Rock, Ark., in the Ozark Natl. Forest; 6 hrs. S of Kansas City, Mo.

RUNNING SEASON: Suggested late March through mid-June.

"Boy, I'll bet these hillbillies don't have a hairy stretch of river in their whole state. I've paddled these streams all spring and . . . " Just about then you funnel down a steep flume bending around a large lichen-covered rock into the Cascade of Extinction. A line of frothy haystacks fling you to the outside of a curve and set you down neatly in the trough of a small but effective hydraulic that comes in from the side at a forty-five-degree angle. It does the trick, and you perform a classic upstream roll as your brace collapses in a pile of foam. Truly humiliated, you sweep down into the willow thicket lining a side eddy and feel a Kansas City lawyer (some "hillbilly") clutch your shoulders and haul you into his Grumman like a dead fish. From along the eddy shore you hear the snickers that more than repay your week of snide remarks about the "whitewaterless Ozarks."

The Big Piney Creek (not to be confused with the Big Piney River in Missouri) is one of the toughest Ozark streams and is for experienced paddlers only. It is small and often constricted even more by gravel shoals and unusually large boulders jutting out from the shoreline. These create steep, swift flumes that often reach top speed just as they turn a corner. The ever-present danger of a downed hickory tree or overhanging willow branch must be guarded against.

But, for the most part, the Big Piney's rapids are remarkably forgiving, both for the upright paddler and the dumped swimmer. The chutes generally have few rocks and usually sweep into calm, flat pools. The tight, tricky rock gardens present the danger of trapping your foot beneath the surface if you attempt to wade, feet down, to shore. This is an unusual hazard for this area, and Big Piney boaters should beware.

For experienced boaters within reach of the Ozarks, this is the river to challenge. And if you feel you are ready for something more than the standard float trips down the Current, Buffalo, and Jacks Fork, try the Big Piney. Just make sure that on this creek, as on any challenging whitewater run, you have a mentor—experienced in rescue as well as paddling technique.

SAN MARCOS RIVER
*The water is mild, the paddlers competent,
the rocks easily seen. But there is something wrong with
this picture. If you can't spot it, you shouldn't be
paddling white water.*

GUADALUPE RIVER
Clue to above problem: The open boaters (above) swamping in a curler and the paddlers (below) lining up for a small drop have all done at least one thing right.

Buffalo River

CLASS: 1+–2
DESCRIPTION: Small; current continuous, but with varying speeds; sluices; some rock gardens.
STANDARD RUN: Put in at Ponca, Ark. (above Ozark Natl. Forest); 18 mi. to take-out at Pruitt.
LOCATION: 3 hrs. NW of Little Rock, Ark.
RUNNING SEASON: Possible all year round; suggested February to May.

New Year's Day. To most avid paddlers this day signifies a terrible hangover or (to the truly fanatic) weight training and jogging. Either way, it's the dead low of the off-season. But for the Ozark Wilderness Waterways Club members, this is the traditional day to be on the water, running the Buffalo. The river has not crested yet, as it will in mid-spring, but the level is quite high and makes a much better run than in bug-infested mid-June, when wading and portaging the shallows is a frequent problem.

Those who have paddled other Ozark streams will find the upper section of the Buffalo unusually rocky. The stream is also narrow and quite winding. The sharp turns, combined with short- to medium-length rock gardens often demand quick technical maneuvering. These Class-2 rocky rapids offer an exciting challenge to the experienced boater, particularly where the river narrows and suddenly accelerates. If you are one of the many beginners who attempt the Buffalo, the unexpected rocks lurking in these swift chutes can spell disaster.

The most legendary of these hazards is Grey Rock. Dropping twenty feet in approximately a hundred yards, you zigzag down a staircase rapid, picking each slot carefully. Then, dropping to the final chute, get set to ride it into the flat pool just around the corner. Suddenly, as you make the turn, a huge twenty-ton boulder looms into view—dead center in the chute. To finish upright, you need a calm bowman with a split-second draw stroke. A warning sign now marks the start of Grey Rock, and it is neither necessary nor advisable to run it blind. On the Buffalo—or any river you run for the first time—scouting should be an inherent part of paddling.

Though it is narrow and relatively rocky, the Buffalo is a typical Ozark stream. The gravel bars offer the paddler a private driftwood-covered campground. High bluffs alternate with low banks covered with oak and hickory. The Buffalo is a "National River," a designation that protects both banks from further development for the entire length of the river. Thus, for the most part, long stretches of forest are interrupted only by grassy farmland.

Flash flooding is another Ozark feature of the Buffalo. One local expert tells of a night when the water rose forty feet and his entire party had to scramble from their gravel bar up to a farmer's field. Within just two days, they were back to wading their boats across shoals and praying for three more inches of water.

LLANO RIVER
Rocks below and bluffs above. A solo paddler picks his way down the Llano at the end of the season.

Current River

CLASS: 1

DESCRIPTION: Broad; slow but continuous current; shallow with riffles and gravel bars; some chutes.

STANDARD RUN: Put in at Montauk State Park, Mo.; 35 mi. to Rte. 19, 51 mi. more to Rte 60, 20 mi. more to Howes Landing, 19 mi. more to Currentview.

LOCATION: 6 hrs. SE of Kansas City, Mo., in Mark Twain Natl. Forest.

RUNNING SEASON: February through late November. Some years runnable all year round.

The dubious honor for the most-paddled stream goes to the Current River. During the summer months liveries with canoes stacked like cordwood send thousands of paddlers onto the Current every weekend. One paddler has counted five hundred boats being launched from a single put-in within two hours on a July Saturday. But by late September the crowds have almost evaporated, and the broad but winding stretches of this long river have a way of swallowing up the few groups of autumn boaters.

Part of the Current's popularity stems from its being a forgiving stream. For most of the 139 miles between Montauk and Currentview, the slow but always continuous current flows over very few large rocks. The gravel bottom makes most rapids merely shoal riffles and unobstructed sluices running between constricted banks. The novice who dumps is in very little danger of being pinned, being swept into a hydraulic, or of losing his boat. Other than plowing into a gravel bar, however, there is one definite danger: downed trees. Water racing around the outside of a curve can erode the bank under the roots, and these "soup strainers" invariably surprise the paddler as he turns the corner.

The ideal campsite for Current paddlers is a convenient sprawling gravel bar on the inside of a curve, just opposite a high sandstone bluff. These bars are usually covered with driftwood from the oaks, maples, and sycamores that line the Current's banks. Though gravel-bar camping is pleasantly open and chigger-free, flooding can be a real hazard. A good rain can raise this stream thirty feet overnight, and many a paddler has found himself scrambling for high ground at midnight, dragging wads of sopping gear. (The rule is always to leave yourself a way out.)

Despite its overpopularity, the Current retains a beautifully pristine character. Over 70 percent of the river's volume comes from huge springs that surface as vast pools and flow into the river as side tributaries. The paddler should stop and hike these spring flows to their source; they are not far from the bank, and the sight of Big Spring pumping over 800,000 gallons per minute is breathtaking.

A MIRACLE OF RARE DEVICE . . .
An oversize folding kayak is powered by sitting paddlers wielding canoe blades. Despite the unique craft, they seem to be faring far better than their swimming cohorts.

NORTH CENTRAL

The mental map of the North Central region, even for widely traveled boaters, remains a vague blur. But hidden away amid remote and endless stands of virgin pine flows some of the nation's most unique and exciting white water.

Streams are generally short, small, but incredibly dynamic. Flat Class 1+ water turns a sharp, blind corner and suddenly plunges six or twelve feet straight down onto a long, tight boulder patch, funneling into a staircase of four vertical ledges that calmly wash out onto a nice Class-1 stretch.

This is not a land of classic rapids. Any of the prevalent waterfalls and ledges *may* drop into a broad pool with a steady hydraulic, or it may just as easily crash onto a mass of boulders swarming with cross currents. Boat-busting rapids abound, and continuous boulder gardens choke most rivers, calling for fast technical paddling.

Boaters new to the area should seek out an experienced guide and expect to do *a lot* of scouting. North Central rivers are extremely unpredictable. Class-2 rapids at the put-in may mask a mile of Class 4 around the bend. Certainly not all of this region's rivers are death defying, but they do demand that the paddler be aware of the unexpected.

The whitewater season is cold and short. Ice doesn't generally break until early April and runoff lasts only until the end of June. Fall rains usually afford some runable levels in September and October. Despite the short season, all types of paddling are popular, from light cruising to intense slalom and wildwater racing. One final advantage: Many of the popular North Central whitewater rivers are protected by state and federal law and afford remote, scenic beauty, rich in wildlife.

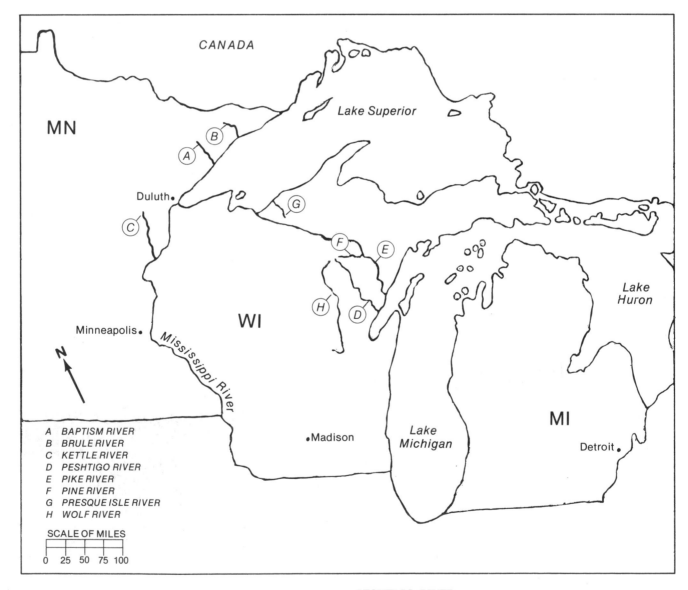

A BAPTISM RIVER
B BRULE RIVER
C KETTLE RIVER
D PESHTIGO RIVER
E PIKE RIVER
F PINE RIVER
G PRESQUE ISLE RIVER
H WOLF RIVER

SCALE OF MILES

0 25 50 75 100

PESHTIGO RIVER
Buried in foam up to his armpits (opposite) a kayakist skirts the edge of a churning keeper hole above him and powers his way downstream.

Peshtigo River

CLASS: 3–4

DESCRIPTION: Powerful, continuous current; few pools; long rock gardens with several ledges.

STANDARD RUN: Put in at Farm Dam site (Wisc.), 4 mi. up County Hwy. C from take-out; 4 mi. to County Hwy. C bridge just above Cauldron Falls Reservoir.

LOCATION: 4 hrs. N of Milwaukee, Wisc.

RUNNING SEASON: April to early June.

If you are one of those paddlers who seeks the security of a well-laid out river with nice V-shaped chutes, a regular series of standing waves, and properly calm side eddies, stay away from the Peshtigo. There is nothing clear-cut about this stream. For four rocky miles, a heavy, very deceptive current flows over steep ledges and long boulder beds creating spiky little waves that just don't seem to follow all those classic water-reading proverbs.

Starting out with a tight, mile-long, Class-2 boulder bed, the Peshtigo swiftly crescendoes to a series of three riverwide ledges. From this point on, resting pools are sparse and short. The final ledge, Third Drop, funnels you immediately into Five-Foot Falls, where you punch through a hydraulic, weave between several boulders, and zig over to the narrow break in the falls, drop five feet, and come up dodging rocks.

But the real myths of the Peshtigo invariably center around Horserace Rapids, where vertical rock walls drastically constrict the river making a heavy-water sleigh ride at breakneck speed. Many an experienced intermediate has scouted this triple-ledge drop and portaged it without regret. Despite its popularity the Peshtigo is a dangerous river. The swift current, continuous flow, and masses of boulders make this a prime area for boat pinning or foot trapping. In addition, the steepness of the rapids makes visibility poor and scouting necessary. But if you have the skill, the Peshtigo is an exciting challenge that combines some heavy water with a natural slalom course.

PESHTIGO RIVER

"Oh, my Gawd!" Pure terror claims another kayaker as he peels out into the infamous Horse Race Rapids.

PESHTIGO RIVER
The holes on a rocky river like the Pesh are not to be trifled with. One paddler (above) tries to punch through and head downstream while (below) another decides to peel out into one and play.

Wolf River

CLASS: *Langlade (Lower Section)*—3. *Hollister (Upper Section)*—2

DESCRIPTION: *Langlade (Lower Section)*—Long, tight, rocky rapids; ledges mixed with boulder gardens; strong tricky current, but not heavy water. *Hollister (Upper Section)*—Not overly steep rock gardens and a few drops; milder, more open version of lower section.

STANDARD RUN: Put in at Hollister, Wisc. (gravel road goes W from town); 9 mi. to Rte. 64 at Langlade, 14 mi. more to Menominee Co. Hwy. WW bridge.

LOCATION: 4 hrs. N of Madison or Milwaukee, Wisc.

RUNNING SEASON: April through June; summer runs dependent on water level.

Just about every tree you see along the river banks of America is second growth—except on the Langlade section of the Wolf. The dark, cold waters of this river flow through several stands of huge virgin pine along the old Menominee Indian Reservation. Protected by the National Wild and Scenic Rivers Act, this remains one of the most beautiful and remote streams in the region.

If you get nothing else out of the Wolf, you will come away with faster reactions. Rapids like Twenty Day, Boy Scout, and Gillmore's Mistake demand sharp maneuvering through long, very tight boulder gardens and constricted drops over hard-to-read ledges. For the most part, this is not a playing stream. It's darn cold, deceptive cross-currents often provide sudden flips, and the rapids are too rock-laced to allow spinning.

However, about halfway through the run there is a very playable exception called Slalom Course Rapids, or Hanson's Rips, where the river con-stricts, forming nice bouncy haystacks and surfable holes. Another surfing favorite is the riverwide curler above Gilmore's Mistake. The only penalty for falling off this wave is the chance of being swept over the sloping ledge just downstream.

There exists a breed of paddler too rough, tough, and stupid ever to scout a rapid, even on a stream like the Wolf with sharp turns and steep ledges. For such jackasses, as well as for the average unfortunate, a large block-and-tackle rig hangs permanently from a tree over Shotgun Rapids to serve as a reminder. It also aids with rescue and has salvaged many a wrapped Grumman.

The run from Hollister to Route 64 is basically a less severe, more open version of the lower run. Mostly Class 2, the river winds over a few nameless drops and through some not-too-steep rock gardens. There are some long flat stretches that on a less scenic river would be uninspiring.

Although it lacks the virgin timber of the lower section, this wilderness run remains thickly wooded with tall pine and some hardwood in its second growth from the lumbering in the 1870s. For the last part of the nineteenth century the Wolf River served as a logging highway, floating timber out to the mills of Green Bay.

For the instructor looking to train novices, this is an ideal run. The river acts as a warm-up, with the rapids getting closer and more intense as you move downstream. Or if you're an open boater, the last two and one-half miles form a downriver racecourse, which used to be run every May with a hilariously jumbling gang start.

Pike River

CLASS: 2–2+

DESCRIPTION: Narrow to medium width; shoaly riffles and long flat stretches; several scoutable drops; few rocks.

STANDARD RUN: Put in from U.S. 141 bridge at Amberg, Wisc.; 10 mi. to take-out just below Yellow Bridge and Pike River Rd.

LOCATION: 4½ hrs. N of Milwaukee, Wisc.; 1½ hrs. N of Green Bay, Wisc.

RUNNING SEASON: Late April through October (occasionally too shallow for summer runs).

The Pike is custom-made for the first-season paddler who wants to get the feel of current beneath his boat and practice some basic maneuvering on an interesting but forgiving stream. Aside from a few short, easily portaged trouble spots, the rapids consist mainly of shallow, swirly riffles weaving between shoals and occasional boulders. It is an unusually open river for this area, yet the current is strong enough to force decisions out of a beginning bowman and make him realize that missing a rock depends entirely on his draw.

Interrupting the short- to medium-length rapids are long flat stretches that offer a chance to enjoy the endless stands of tall jack pine, white pine, and poplar that grow down to the river's edge. Although there is some farmland, most of this run flows through permanently protected forest and gives a true wilderness feeling. In addition, the shallow side eddies are full of the fish that named this river.

Along with the Class-1 practice runs, the Pike is spiced with several short, steep Class-2 sections that present the beginner with a strong whitewater challenge. A mile from the put-in, Powerline Rapids confronts the boater with an unusually steep boulder bed that demands some tight rock dodging. Horseshoe Ledge funnels the paddler over a two-foot drop into a small curler. Crooked Bull Falls, or Yellow Bridge Rapids, is a double ledge requiring a sharp zigzag. Fortunately these and the other serious trouble spots can be easily read from above, and all have convenient portage trails.

Pine River

CLASS: 1–2

DESCRIPTION: Narrow, winding, shallow; short-to-medium-length rock gardens; occasional low drops and chutes.

STANDARD RUN: Put in at Chipmunk Rapids Campground, Wisc. (via dirt road off Rte. 70); 9 mi. to Goodman Grade, 9 mi. more to U.S. 141.

LOCATION: 5 hrs. N of Milwaukee, Wisc.; just below Wisc.-Mich. border near Iron Mountain, Mich.

RUNNING SEASON: April to July; occasionally in early fall.

In 1965 Wisconsin's Pine River, along with the neighboring Pike and Popple rivers, were declared "Wild Rivers" and came under the permanent protection of the state. A massive campaign to raise funds, buy land outright, and obtain scenic easements was launched. Today, the fight still continues, but most of the land surrounding the Pine, Popple, and Pike river valleys in the northeast corner of Wisconsin has been saved from further commercial development.

Thus this section of the Pine and the less frequently paddled stretch starting twenty miles upstream run through beautiful near-wilderness. Thick stands of pine with sprinklings of aspen and birch line the shores in endless, unbroken stretches.

In early spring the paddler should watch the eddies for deer, Canadian geese and other waterfowl, and even an occasional beaver.

The Pine is a narrow winding stream with most of the rapids formed by short rock gardens that require definite but not drastic maneuvering. Between rapids long stretches of flat alternate with shoaly riffles, letting you enjoy the scenery while still feeling a moving current. But don't grow too lackadaisical drifting and drinking in the scenery. Some interesting Class-2+ challenges can surprise you on this river. In several places the river volume constricts, forming foot-high haystacks and pitching over one or several ledges. These constricted drops, such as Snake Tail, Meyers Falls, and Bulls Falls rapids, can mean a fun sleigh ride for some or an unexpected dump for the unwary.

The run from Chipmunk Campground to Route 141 makes a scenic and leisurely trip. Take the weekend and camp along the river, fish for rainbows, sit by the campfire at night, and listen for coyotes and barred and snowy owls amidst the endless ripple of the water. Enjoy one of America's all-too-few wild rivers.

WOLF RIVER
"Yaah-HOOO!" With a joyous ferocity, Bronze medalist Al Button (opposite) powers his home-designed C-1, C-Gull, from wave crest to wave crest.

POWERHOUSE AND SON

Wildwater C-1 Bronze medalist Al Button and his son (above) drive their C-2 through the gates at the St. Croix slalom race.

KETTLE RIVER

On a flat, sunlit stretch (below) a beginner receives instruction. She will continue through her flatwater apprenticeship before hitting white water.

FURTHER DOWNSTREAM ON THE KETTLE

A C-1 and two C-2s (opposite) cruise through this Class-2 + section amid forests of evergreen and white birch.

Presque Isle River

CLASS: 4–5 (closed boat)

DESCRIPTION: Incredible. Heavy continuous water; high ledges; big holes; very swift.

STANDARD RUN: Put in from Rte. 28, (midway between Wakefield and Bergland, Mich.); 5 mi. to Minnewawah Falls (via logging road off Rte. 28), 7 mi. more to Porcupine Mtns. Rd. in Porcupine Mtns. State Park.

LOCATION: Ottawa Natl. Forest, NW corner of Michigan's Upper Peninsula; 6 hrs. N of Madison, Wisc.

RUNNING SEASON: Late April to early June, September and October.

"Well," said a Michigan paddler, "It's like your Gauley, only a lot harder." The West Virginia boater glowered, muttered something about turkeys from the North through clenched teeth. Firm regional prejudice demands such useless comparisons; each man staunchly believes that *his* area has the toughest, most demanding water. But boasts and lies aside, the Presque Isle is about the meanest water North Central can offer.

This recently discovered, experts-only run can begin from the Route 28 bridge. Starting here offers a five-mile warm-up of Class-3-to-4 drops and boulder patches separated by substantial pools. Most boaters, preferring to skip this and get right into the action, put in just below Minnewawah Falls. If the upper section scared you, this will eat you alive. For the next seven miles an incredibly swift, powerful current twists its way around sharp, blind curves and plunges over four-to-twelve foot falls, and into holes tailor-made for unintentional enders. These falls, like Nimkon, Triple Drop, Conglomerate Staircase, are actually a complex series of ledges that can drop you twelve feet in two or three not-so-easy stages into a hydraulic. Tight maneuvering and sharp water reading are demanded, since these riverwide ledges follow each other so closely.

The Presque Isle is a dangerous river. Blind curves hide little surprises that no amount of expertise can avoid. A four-foot-thick downed tree, hiding around a curve at the bottom of Nakomis Falls, makes a death trap in all but the lowest levels. One hundred and fifty yards from the take-out a huge tree jam waits to swallow the unwary. Run this river with someone who has done it before and plan to scout.

But it's not all a series of gut-wrenching drops with Indian names even the locals can't pronounce. There are long exhilarating sleigh rides where the boater plunges through continuous standing waves, weaving between the holes. For the expert, the Presque Isle offers an ideal combination of top-end challenge and just plain heavy-water fun, a combination, guaranteed to produce what one expert wistfully calls "whitewater euphoria."

WOLF RIVER
Al Button punches his way through a hole in his downriver C-1 and works to rejoin the mainstream.

PESHTIGO RIVER
(above and below) *The ups and downs of slalom competition. Just surviving this river demands skill and courage, but to run it and successfully maneuver between the red-and-green poles demands true expertise.*

Kettle River

CLASS: 2+−3+

DESCRIPTION: Broad, big river; moving flat stretches alternate with sharp drops and chutes.

STANDARD RUN: Put in at Rte. 23 bridge, off Rte. 35 (Minn.); 5 mi. to take-out at Sandstone (just under RR bridge).

LOCATION: 2 hrs. N of Minneapolis–St. Paul, Minn.

RUNNING SEASON: June through October; during April and May rapids become Class 4.

"A piece of cake," you think. "It's gotta be." Standing by the car, untying your K-1, you look down the long stretch of slow, totally placid water by the put-in. The topo map indicates the Kettle drops only twenty feet per mile, and you start to wonder if it's all worth it.

What you don't know, but are soon to learn indelibly, is that virtually all of those twenty feet occur in two or three spots every mile. The Kettle is a classic pool-and-plunge river. Half a mile below that deceptive put-in lurks Blueberry Slide, where a large granite slab funnels most of the river volume into a steep left chute with haystacks and a strong stopper hole in high water.

Water level means everything on the Kettle. It's a wide stream and, at most of the major drops, the river narrows considerably, turning that little ledge you scraped over last July into a real 3+ hydraulic in early spring. Dragon's Tooth is a perfect example. The river narrows to about thirty feet between high, vertical sandstone bluffs. The whole river pitches through this canyon into a minefield of stopper holes. At low summer levels, you can punch through these holes—just barely. Other times they will recycle boat and paddler for a month. In addition, higher levels hide the undercut canyon wall, which has lethal possibilities.

But don't get too frightened. The Kettle is a very pleasant intermediate stream with rapids seldom above Class 2+ in summer runs. The individual boater must merely beware of running it too early in the spring for his skill level. As a final lure, several of the steep rapids have long chutes that trail into wide pools and are excellent for wave surfing, snap eddies, and hole playing.

Baptism River

CLASS: 2–6 (closed boat)

DESCRIPTION: Hairy! Narrow, twisty, tight; swift current, many ledges and drops, several unrunnable falls.

STANDARD RUN: Put in at East or West Branch either side of Finland, Minn. (less than a mile to confluence); 6 mi. to Illgen Falls (trail leads to State Rte. 1), 3 mi. more to Rte. 61 and Lake Superior.

LOCATION: 1+ hr. NE of Duluth, Minn., along shore of Lake Superior.

RUNNING SEASON: Late April to June; sometimes possible in September and October.

The Baptism is a wild river in every sense of the word. Few rivers instill so dramatically the beauty, energy, and power of free-flowing water as this north-shore stream. Within the first six miles Avalanche and Illgen Falls pour over rugged basalt ledges, plunging vertically twenty-five to thirty feet into a white mass of mist and foam. As you portage these unrunnable drops, you abandon all fantasies about battling the power of the current.

Except for these two falls the rest of the run is survivable by experts and advanced intermediates. It starts out with a long and pleasant Class-2 boulder garden that is a great warm-up for the drops to come. Past the Eckbeck campground at Route 1 the ledges come hard and fast. Truck-size boulders and

sharp twists around wooded corners make visibility poor and scouting essential. Confinement Canyon and Kraemers Revenge both reach their climax while you are making sharp turns.

The Baptism River is on the edge of the BWCA (Boundry Water Canoe Area), and the wilderness scenery is some of the most magnificent in the country. Thick, dark woods of pine and aspen, lightened by an occasional birch hide bear, beaver, and even a rare wolf. This north-shore area is about as close to wilderness as you can come in a weekend trip.

But the most awesome scenery occurs on the remaining three miles below the standard take-out at Illgen Falls. If you are an energetic expert with a willingness to make incredibly steep portages, this section is just barely runnable. For the less intrepid there is a hiking trail along the canyon's edge that follows back up from U.S. 61. Either way you will view the highest and most spectacular falls in the state. High Falls plunges eighty-five vertical feet, the highest waterfall in Minnesota. The Cascades fall sixty feet down along a granite crevasse. To the casual hiker these and other falls of this section are impressive. But to the whitewater paddler there is an awe-inspiring sense of power that only he can feel.

Brule River

CLASS: 4–5 (with some unrunnable sections; *closed boat*)

DESCRIPTION: Broad; swift heavy current; boulder patches long with big rocks; several ledges.

STANDARD RUN: Put in at end of County Road 70 (off U.S. 61 and County Road 69 in Minn.), portage ½ mi. to Brule River Sauna Bath Rapids; 7 mi. to take-out at U.S. 61 and shore of Lake Superior.

LOCATION: 2½ hrs. NE of Duluth, Minn. (along coast of Lake Superior).

RUNNING SEASON: April to mid-June; occasional fall runs depending on water level.

If anyone ever boasts he has run *all* of the Brule, do not believe it. Devil's Kettle is probably the most unrunnable rapid God ever designed. The entire river bends sharply to the right and funnels over a sheer forty-foot drop caroming off the vertical walls of a constricting stone canyon. About twenty feet down on the right side, most of the water disappears into the swirling maelstrom of the Kettle. Legend has it that years back a group of researchers (more interested in studying rivers than damming them) dropped a barrel of red dye into that vortex and it later mushroomed up in the middle of Lake Superior.

Most of the Brule's remaining seven miles lies well within human capability. For experts and experienced intermediates, it represents a classic in tight, technical maneuvering. Immediately after putting in, the paddler plunges right into Sauna Bath Rapids, weaving his way through a complex web of huge boulders, which hide a minefield of keeper holes. These long boulder gardens spiced with occasional ledgy drops continue the entire length of the river. The most delightful section is the three-by-three Flume—three miles of nonstop Class-3 water with enough rock dodging to be challenging but not nerve-racking. Toward the end, the challenge increases, particularly in Brule Canyon, where the boater is constantly trying to decide which holes he can punch through and which he has to scramble like mad to avoid.

If you have any remaining energy after rock dodging for seven continuous miles and portaging around the unrunnables—Devil's Kettle, Canyon Falls, and Upper Falls—you can surf to your heart's content in the waves of Lake Superior.

RACE PREPARATION

First you don your wet suit, spray skirt, life jacket, and helmet. Then you pick up your boat from what looks like a fiberglass junk yard.

WEST

Mention Western rivers to almost any paddler and his eyes sparkle as he conjures up images of horrendous water hurtling downstream at twenty mph filled with terrifying haystacks and huge, raft-swallowing holes. This stereotype is not without justification. From the steep sides of the Continental Divide flow swift, continuous, unimpeded rivers with some of the nation's biggest white water. Unlike the Appalachians with their boulder-laced streams, the younger, more intact Rockies claim more open and less rock-hindered rivers. So, while the paddler is battling bigger and faster water, the obstacles tend to be widely spaced holes rather than tightly packed rocks.

Although the huge-volume stereotype is renowned, it is not universal. There is an endless variety of white water within the region and even in each river. For example, the Snake River, which hurtles kayakers and rafters through Hell's Canyon in Idaho, also carries open boaters along incredibly swift, deceptively flat and open stretches in Wyoming. On some of these flat, fast rivers, the canoe camper can cover twenty miles before lunch. On others the water erupts into a technical rapids as it passes through massive boulder gardens formed by the house-size talus broken off from canyon walls.

The popular season for most Western rivers is from mid-May through September, with peak levels from early to mid-July. While the air is warm, the snowmelt rivers are often quite cold. But as hydroelectric needs grow, more of this region's rivers are becoming dam controlled. While this lengthens the season for some streams, it also floods out some of the nicest, most popular rivers.

In order to lessen the environmental impact, the state and federal forest services issue a very limited number of paddling permits for many popular rivers. Applications must be submitted to the forest service by late fall if you hope to make a spring or summer run.

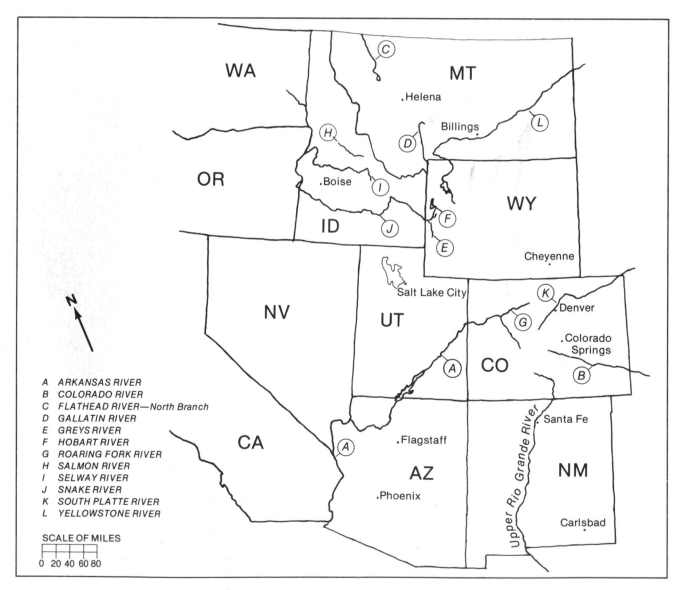

A ARKANSAS RIVER
B COLORADO RIVER
C FLATHEAD RIVER—North Branch
D GALLATIN RIVER
E GREYS RIVER
F HOBART RIVER
G ROARING FORK RIVER
H SALMON RIVER
I SELWAY RIVER
J SNAKE RIVER
K SOUTH PLATTE RIVER
L YELLOWSTONE RIVER

SCALE OF MILES
0 20 40 60 80

COLORADO RIVER
(opposite) *Rafting through the Grand, or any of this river's other canyons, provides a unique perspective that is closed to all but the paddling visitor.*

South Platte River

CLASS: *Upper Run—1-2+. Lower Run* (Waterton Canyon)—4-5

DESCRIPTION: *Upper Run*—Short, shoaly rapids alternating with meandering flat; open easy current. *Lower Run*—Narrow and swift; half continuous drops and rocks followed by half flat.

STANDARD RUN: Deckers, Colo., off Rte. 67. *Upper Run*—21 mi. to town of South Platte. *Lower Run*—12 mi. more to Waterton. *Slalom course:* Mid-Denver downstream of Waterton.

LOCATION: 1 hr. SW of Denver, Colo.

RUNNING SEASON: Late May through October. Dam releases make lower section crest in July and August. Slalom course runnable all year.

If you live in Denver and want to give whitewater a try, nothing could be more convenient than the South Platte. This easy, forgiving learners' river provides all the action of beginning whitewater on a roadside run that allows the neophyte to tackle as long a hunk of river as his muscles can handle with very few penalties for his mistakes.

A narrow river, the South Platte runs over low, shoaly drops that demand definite decision making and coordination between bow and stern. These short rapids usually contain one or two major obstacles in a constricted current, but they never become overly technical. The great boat dumper in this section is a tight, vertical drop called the Slot. If you line your boat up with the current at the top of the rapid, it's a short but sweet sluice. If not, you may sweep broadside and suddenly be dumped upstream. The only other obstacles are the children who like to dive into the foot of the rapid from low side cliffs.

Although it is near Denver, the run is actually quite scenic. Small stands of willow and pine line the grassy banks, occasionally broken by verdant farmland. When you see a new paddler on the South Platte's slalom course in downtown Denver, there's a good chance he got his first taste of whitewater on the Deckers–to–South Platte run.

For a half mile beyond South Platte, the river continues much as it had in the upstream run: flat with some riffles. Then upon entering Waterton Canyon, the river suddenly and dramatically changes to six solid miles of Class 4. The volume is still small, 350 to 750 cfs make an optimum run, with 1,000 being hazardous. But the constricted flow, rushing over steep, tight rock-studded cascades for six miles makes the Waterton Canyon a run for experts and very advanced intermediates.

About three miles into the canyon a four-foot concrete weir tempts the boater, but a concrete shelf and large cylindrical water conduit lurk at bottom, just aching to gobble up any floating fiberglass. Scout this one. But the real legends of this run blossom around the Widow-maker, a rock-choked S turn with huge haystacks and irregular holes. A complex Class 3 at 350 cfs, it rages to 5 at 750 and above. A foamy pattern of crisscrossing tongues shunt the boater from rock to rock, and even after scouting (very mandatory), you can still get slammed into a rock wall.

These six continuous miles of Class 4 carry the boater just a touch past halfway point and out onto a long stretch of flattish backwash. Two dams approximately two miles apart create four miles of sluggish or totally still water. Below the second dam a small creeklike runout leads two more miles to the take-out. The level of this stretch should be checked from the road, since it often shallows out, making the last two miles a boat-towing wade.

LABYRINTH CANYON—GREEN RIVER
(below) *Although this scenic stretch of the Green is flat, heavy helmet-and-life jacket water lies in wait further downstream.*

PILE-UP
(opposite)*Rocks are not the paddler's only obstacle. River etiquette demands you leave ample room between boats, but unfortunately the river doesn't always help.*

Arkansas River—Upper

CLASS: 3 + –5

DESCRIPTION: Heavy, powerful, varied; huge holes, large boiling water; long rapids; some above-surface large rocks.

STANDARD RUN: Put in at Lake Creek, N of Riverside, Colo., off Rte. 24; 4 mi. through Pine Creek Canyon to Scotts Bridge, 10 mi. more to Buena Vista.

LOCATION: 3½ hrs. SW of Denver, Colo.; 76 miles W of Colorado Springs, Colo.

RUNNING SEASON: May through September.

Everyone who paddles the Arkansas loves it. Wide-eyed boasts, such as "Supreme whitewater river," "best in the state," are constantly heard in paddlers' enthusiastic descriptions. From Coloradans, often considered to have the best whitewater state in the nation, such superlatives are high praise, indeed. But the Arkansas is worthy: For nearly one hundred miles it offers long varied sections of terrifying, large volume "hair," blended with easier, more playable, heavy-water fun.

The Pine Creek Canyon run is definitely in the hair category. Putting in at Lake Creek confluence, the boater immediately confronts Pine Creek rapids. He chutes over a ten-foot nearly vertical drop and keeps steadily plunging 250 feet down over one and a-half miles. For the solid 5+ expert, it is a gut-wrenching, top-end challenge. For anyone less, it is insanity.

In high water the Arkansas becomes a monstrous flush. Incredibly swift flumes sweep you down through a litter of yawning holes and wandering hydraulics. These are the kinds of rapids where you can literally fall off a tongue, drop several feet into a massive hole, get recycled end over end, and be spit out into a boiling mass of countercurrents. Although most of the rapids are straight shots, provided you avoid some holes, the sheer size of the water is awesome and can cause even top paddlers to freeze up. In lower water, the canyon is still horrendous, but some of those mushrooming boilers turn to eddies, and several large, river-constricting rock piles become exposed jetties rather than a single long hydraulic.

For the last two and one half miles of the run, the river suddenly reins back and slows to Class 2. Here, as in the rapids upstream, there are several constrictions caused by the boulders dumped into the river when the road through the canyon was built. This stretch affords the paddler a chance to view the rugged bare rock of the steep canyon walls, with their countless strata of rich reds and browns.

Coming to Scotts Bridge, which those not quite up to the canyon can use as a put-in, the river broadens slightly, flattening out for several hundred yards. Then approximately nine miles above Buena Vista, the paddler comes upon the American Canoe Association training site. It is not always in use, but when it is, it is a great place to swap information or work the slalom gates that hang much of the year.

From here the advanced intermediate can make the Big Six Rapids run into Buena Vista. Six moderately steep, Class-4 rapids provide excellent playing holes and huge surfing waves. Generally, the rapids are long, with enough small boulders to keep the maneuvering interesting but never tight. Although the Bix Six gives this section a pool-and-plunge feeling, the river never stops. The short, swift-moving flat stretches that follow each rapid all too quickly flow into the Class-2 lead-in riffles of the next drop.

The Arkansas is one of the few popular, heavy whitewater streams in the Colorado area that requires no permit and that is free of commercial rafters. So though it lacks the wilderness aura of the Grand and the Selway, at least you don't have to wait in line.

Arkansas River—Lower

CLASS: 3–4+

DESCRIPTION: Medium width, very swift; large rocks and huge haystacks broken by continuous moving flat.

STANDARD RUN: Put in at Parkdale, Colo. (off Rte. 50); 8 mi. through Royal Gorge to Canon City (Class 4+).

UPSTREAM RUNS: *Browns Canyon:* Put in at Buena Vista, Colo.; 10 mi. to Rte. 165 take-out at Nanthrop. Put in at Salida, Colo.; 25 mi. to Cotopaxi take-out at Rte. 50 (Class 3).

LOCATION: 2½ hrs. SW of Denver, Colo.; 36 mi. W of Pueblo, Colo.

RUNNING SEASON: Suggested May through September.

In January, 1878, two railroads stood poised at the mouth of the Royal Gorge, the last tight canyon on the Arkansas before it leaves the mountains and rushes out onto the plains. Upstream, at the river's headwaters, Leadville, the West's largest mining boomtown, rich and stranded, was screaming for service. The Santa Fe Railroad, headed by the infamous Jay Gould, locked horns with the western line: the Denver and Rio Grande. It was a standard railroad battle: an exhaustive courtroom fight, threats and commissions of mutual violence, and vast congressional bribings. In the end Leadville's impatient miners built their own freight road across Mosquito Pass, linking up with another line. Eventually, Denver got the Royal Gorge, and Gould's Santa Fe struggled across Raton Pass.

Today it's tourists rather than mine ore that pack the Royal Gorge's forty-five degree inclined railway to glide down the sheer thousand-foot walls of pink granite. Though the tourist value of this beautifully scenic canyon is thoroughly exploited, from the railway to the Royal Gorge suspension bridge swaying 1,055 feet above the river, the boater senses none of this invasion.

Between the vertical granite walls, he paddles for eight continuous miles on a swift 4+ stream surging with surprising force. Large, thirty-five-foot boulders choke the flow, making winding series of huge haystacks. The steeply pitched current zigzags across these narrow flumes, ricocheting off boulders and canyon walls. Few of these are undercut, but the incredible speed and force of the river can cause bad slams and pinnings, making even experts ride the inside of the curve. The long rapids spit the boater out into "flat" sections drifting lazily at a mere five to six miles per hour with four-foot haystacks.

Though it's not a tight, technical run, an unusually heavy (for the Arkansas) sprinkling of varied-size holes keeps you maneuvering. Throughout the run, there are two dams that are mandatory portages. (At some levels these drops look runnable, but deceptively powerful recycler holes at the bottom make them dangerous.)

Note: This high-speed, eight-mile run is short, and many groups try to cram in a second run toward late afternoon. Heavy water is exhausting, and that superman exhilaration you feel at the take-out can numb you to your drained muscles. In addition, night falls suddenly and early in this narrow, vertical-walled canyon. The trip leader should know, not guess, the daylight paddling hours, and each individual paddler should know when to quit for his own safety. This is no river to run by braille or when you are half dead with fatigue.

SMILE!

Many paddlers like this one (below) advocate the open-mouth approach: If you can't paddle it, swallow it. (Recommended for short rivers only.)

COLORADO RIVER

Pausing in a narrow, scenic side canyon (opposite), a paddler in his tiny raft basks in a shaft of sunlight and studies the water-etched canyon walls surrounding him.

THE GRAND CANYON
Unless you're an expert decked boater, commercial raft trips are about the only way to experience the canyon's mud-brown heavy water. Depending on the outfitter, you may be expected to help (opposite top) or just be a passenger (opposite center) and hang on. Either way there is plenty of action. A river guide (opposite bottom) pilots his gear- and guest-laden craft through an average-size hole. A large hole can flip these eighteen-foot inflatables end-over-end.

RUBY CANYON—COLORADO RIVER
Upstream of the Grand Canyon, near the Colorado-Utah border (below), paddlers are overwhelmed by huge masses of water-molded granite topped with spires of multi-colored sediment.

Roaring Fork

CLASS: 4–5

DESCRIPTION: Heavy, swift, continuous current; wide with many rocks above and below surface.

STANDARD RUN: Put in at Aspen, Colo., below golf course on Cemetery Lane; 7 mi. to take-out at first Woody Creek bridge. *Class 2:* Put in just below Basalt, Colo., off Rte. 82; 4 mi. to KOA campground; 3 mi. more to Catherine's Store bridge. *Class 2–4:* Put in at Carbondale, Colo., off Rte. 82; 12 mi. to confluence with Colorado River, campground below Glenwood Springs.

LOCATION: 3½ hrs. SW of Denver, Colo.

RUNNING SEASON: Early June through September.

Who says western rivers don't have rocks? Popular scuttlebut by boaters who dash west, run two or three rivers, and then run home has spread the belief that all rivers "out there" are one long bouncy sluice, which you could run broadside and never hit anything solid. But the Roaring Fork Canyon is strewn with all the stones that would make a Connecticut farmer curse and a New England paddler feel right at home.

For seven miles the river flows in one continuous, unbroken rapid descending at a surprisingly steep, constant pitch. The run kicks off with Slaughterhouse Rapids, a six-foot fall that used to power a riverside slaughterhouse. From then on the boater is constantly weaving his way through a tight, technical minefield. In spring the silty brown runoff covers many of the rocks, creating a garden of irregularly shaped, nonplayable holes. Toward July the river drops and becomes clear, and the holes yield to huge chimney-shaped boulders.

The Roaring Fork is a river to run, not play. Both holes and hydraulics are too odd-shaped for really good surfing. Eddies are small and rare. It is an expert-only run where the paddler is always tilting his boat on the side to avoid a rock slamming or giving a quick draw to prevent getting pinned bow and stern. And though the swift current slows slightly in lower levels, many of the larger boulders tower overhead, making water reading nearly impossible. If it's your first run, try to have some mentor who has run it before and plan to do a lot of scouting to avoid paddling down a "dry chute."

The Roaring Fork Canyon, when you have the chance to look, offers magnificent scenery. Sheer cliffs of gray shale marbled with vivid red and yellow strata tightly cloister the river's flow. Sitting in his eddy, watching the rushing waters ceaselessly pound the soft, crumbling stone, the boater senses the impermanence of the canyon and the enormous power of the river as it carves an ever-changing channel. This perspective and the special realization of that power are some of the paddler's unique rewards.

SNAKE RIVER

(below) *Father-and-son competitors race downriver in a decked Grumman. Decks for open boats are available commercially. But they can be expensive, so most are homemade devices.*

COLORADO RIVER

Cruising down the Colorado (opposite) in an eighteen-foot commercial raft calls for skill and an extra hand to hang on with.

Colorado River—Grand Canyon

CLASS: Up to 5+

DESCRIPTION: Broad, heavy, humongous river; long steep cascades, high haystacks; many holes, many long stretches of flat water.

STANDARD RUN: Put in at Lee's Ferry, Ariz., 6 mi. below Lake Powell in Grand Canyon Natl. Park; 225 miles to Diamond Creek Rd. in Hualapai Indian Reservation.

LOCATION: 2 hrs. N of Flagstaff, Ariz. (near Utah border); approx. 650 mi. SW of Denver, Colo. (by highway).

RUNNING SEASON: Permit required. Suggested late April through October; possible all year round.

"Mountains of music swell in the rivers, hills of music billow in the creeks, meadows of music murmur in the rills that ripple over the rocks, while other melodies are heard in the lateral canyons. The Grand Canyon is a land of song."—from the diary of Major John Wesley Powell, 1869, first man to run the canyons of the Colorado

Unfortunately, it is impossible to view the Grand Canyon exactly as the famous one-armed explorer and his ten-man crew did over a century ago: raging naturally, unchecked by concrete dams, and void of all human signs, save a rare long-abandoned Indian settlement. But though today's boater no longer enjoys this untouched perspective, the savagery of this massive river and the majestic beauty of its many-hued canyon walls still remain to awe and inspire the paddler.

The Grand Canyon's rapids, though long and horrendous, are often separated by miles of nearly still flat water. They are mostly caused by affluvial tributaries rushing in from the side or—more seldom—flow-constricting jumbles of rock and silt broken off the canyon wall. So the paddler spends two to three miles nervously anticipating the inevitable, then he hears that menacing low rumble bouncing off the canyon walls, then plunges into a world of whitewater like no other. He sweeps up and screams down around mountainous, fifteen-foot haystacks. Frantically he struggles away from ferryboat-size holes. He squints to read a river so silt-laden that the biggest holes or highest wave crests show none of that familiar, warning white. It is all one chocolate brown mass. The mansion-size boulders are a blessing. The "tongues" are so irregular, so churned with ever-wandering countercurrents, that maneuvering is a constant necessity. All this in water so mammoth no expert ever gets used to it. It's fashionable among experts to say of Lava Falls, House Rock, and other big rapids, "Oh, it's just a straight shot in very big water." Though surface rocks are few, any river filled with moving boilers, ringed with a circular hydraulic, is not just a straight shot. Along Marble, Lava, and Granite Canyons, and the subcanyons that comprise the Grand, nature displays the incredible variety possible where water struggles against stone. Rainbows of ribbonlike strata run across soft sedimentary canyon walls. Blood red or silty brown waterfalls pour in from the side. Vast walls of polished, fluted limestone, smooth arches and cathedrallike spires, piles of reddish-brown talus, dark angular granite dikes slashed with white schist, and water of every conceivable color all combine to make the Grand America's most awesome canyon. It is the one great wonder all Americans should see.

Note: Unfortunately seeing this sight from a paddler's perspective is just slightly easier than obtaining knighthood. Whether you are seeking information for commercial raft or private boat trips write: Inner Canyon Unit Mgr., Grand Canyon Natl. Park, Grand Canyon, Ariz. 86023.

For a private trip plan approximately ten days to Diamond Creek. The trip application demands you totally plan your trip ahead of time.

SALMON RIVER

The superbly sea-worthy dory, once used as a coastal fishing vessel, has recently become a popular whitewater craft. Like a kayak it pivots quickly (above) for upstream ferries and has a high, decked prow for ploughing (opposite top) through the Salmon's huge haystacks.

For those lacking skill in dory or kayak, commercial outfitters (opposite bottom) offer six-day trips down the middle and main forks of the Salmon.

SNAKE RIVER

The Snake is one of the most varied and scenic rivers in the West. Near Cheyenne, Wyoming (center) two paddlers streak down a swift, flat stretch. Rafters watch a competitor (below) in the annual Governor's Cup Race as he powers his wildwater kayak downstream.

Gallatin River

CLASS: 1–2+ (and up to 4 downstream)
DESCRIPTION: Swift, continuous current; narrow, constricted, and windy; relatively rocky at low levels.
STANDARD RUN: Put in at northwest corner of Yellowstone Natl. Park, Mont., along Rte. 191; 60 mi. to Bozeman Hot Springs.
LOCATION: 3½ hrs. SW of Billings, Mont.
RUNNING SEASON: Late May through October.

Back in 1805, when a wild and youthful America swaggered with pride and the new nation's cabinet members enjoyed the same exuberant celebration now reserved for TV heroes, explorer Meriwether Lewis named this energetic stream after Albert Gallatin, U.S. Secretary of the Treasury. This was the third of three parallel rivers flowing north into the Missouri that Lewis and Clark encountered on their return trip eastward. The Madison and Jefferson rivers, to the west, commemorated the president and secretary of state.

Today, the Gallatin offers paddlers sixty miles of gradually accelerating and more difficult whitewater, from its Class-1+ headwaters at the tip of Yellowstone to the advanced intermediate sections near Bozeman Hot Springs. Flowing out of Gallatin Lake in the Washburn Range, the steadily dropping river maintains a very swift, continuous current. For the first twenty miles to the Twin Peaks campground, rapids are seldom above Class 2. But don't be fooled. This deceptively flat, clear water makes up in speed what it lacks in haystacks, and the boater has to adjust his reflexes to this fast, ever-moving river.

In the summer months, the boater is constantly dodging small rounded boulders and gravel bars. But fall and late spring bring higher, more open levels. Past Twin Peaks, small affluvial feeders increase the Gallatin's volume, creating first a sprinkling, then continuous clusters, of Class-3-to-4 sleigh rides. Farther downstream rocks become larger and scarcer, while the river bends increase. And the Gallatin is a convenient river: Route 191 follows the river the entire way, providing limitless access. The paddler just scouts out a suitable stretch and then spots a car at the take-out.

Though never far from the highway, the Gallatin has an open, if not totally wilderness, feeling. Pine and spruce forests alternate with lush meadows and ranch grassland, covering a broad valley floor. The jagged outline of the Madison Range rims the western horizon. National park campsites line both banks, and the eddies are filled with Dolly Varden and Cutthroat for the fishermen. If you are an open-boat cruiser seeking a scenic trip of indefinite length and minimal planning, the Gallatin is your river.

GREEN RIVER
(below) *A few quiet moments to reflect on the massive grandeur of the West.*

LEAN 'N BRACE
A paddler(opposite) hangs upright in a hole by bracing his paddle blade on the water and leaning to present the bottom of his boat to the oncoming current.

Selway River

CLASS: 4–5+

DESCRIPTION: Wide, powerful, fairly continuous; large haystacks and holes; mostly open with some rocky sections.

STANDARD RUN: Put in at McGrouder Ranger Station, Ida.; 48 mi. to confluence with Clearwater River (2 mi. above Selway Falls).

LOCATION: 6 hrs. NE of Boise. Flows between Bitterroot and Nez Perce Natl. Forests.

RUNNING SEASON: Mid-May through early July; August and September runs dependent on spring runoff. Permit required.

The Selway is one of the favorites on the western river baggers' list. We all know river baggers—those prestige-oriented paddlers who every weekend hunt and bag another "name river" to prove they can handle the big stuff. But paddling a dramatic river like the Selway once proves very little. Its ever-changing character demands a different kind of paddling skill in every stretch of the river, every time you paddle it.

Flowing past the McGrouder Ranger Station, it feels like a small winding woods stream with as little as 200 cfs passing by. But countless feeder streams pouring in from either side quickly double and redouble its volume, transforming its character to a broad, raging, typically Idaho river that pours up to a 3,000–4,000 cfs over Selway Falls. In late May, when the put-in gauge reads 7 to 9 feet, the Selway covers most of its rocky sections and creates incredibly swift, tricky tongues that shunt the paddler toward massive recycler holes. During summer, as the gauge drops toward 3.5, overhead rocks rise up out of the holes, and the boater squints to find a totally different set of narrower, more diffuse tongues. Some but not all of the heavy water hole plunging changes to intense rock dodging.

But at any level, it is an expert run where an incredibly swift current sweeps the boater through alternating stretches of broad flushes with heavy haystacks and unavoidable holes; ever-moving flat water; and steep, multichanneled boulder gardens with rocks you have to peer around. Shortly after the put-in, boaters encounter Double Drop. This slanting S-turn, split by a massive, boat-eating hole between drops, introduces paddlers to the horrendous power they will face in the rock-studded Washer Woman and all the way to the falls. At mile 26, Moose Creek enters from the north, nearly doubling the river's volume. Just below rumbles Ladel Rapids, a steep drop off into nowhere with either a riverwide hydraulic or channel-splitting house-size rock, depending on the level. This tricky dangerous rapid must be scouted. If you don't feel utterly confident, you'd better portage the next three-quarters of a mile. The long stretch of Class-4-to-5 rock and hole dodging that follows is no place for a swimmer.

The scenery in the U-shaped canyon of the Selway is as variable as its rapids. The river is located in the Bitterroot Wilderness Area. The banks are generally low, set back, and slanting away from the river. Yet shortly after the Selway joins Moose Creek, the bluffs become steeper and move in, giving a closer feeling to the river for a short way. Large rock talus from crumbling cliffs alternates with heavily wooded slopes of cedar and pine. Carried through a thick forest of huge cedars, two and a half feet in diameter, then suddenly being brought into a barren atmosphere of rock, cliff, and gravel, the paddler realizes the variety nature displayed in just a few miles and the foolishness of generalizing about one state or even one region's geography.

Note: The Selway is usually a two- to three-day trip. Eighteen miles downriver, a nice midway breaking point, the Selway Lodge offers paddlers excellent, though expensive, accommodations. This allows the weekend river runner the advantage of running this Class-5 river with an empty boat.

HOLING UP
(opposite) *One paddler sits in the trough of a hole, battered by a massive roller, while the other uses the upstream curler to surf.*

HIDDEN BOAT TRICK
What looks like a K-2 team (right) is actually two K-1 paddlers churning through a hydraulic.

CONTINUOUS WHITE WATER
(below) *On all levels of difficulty, this is the hallmark of Western paddling. Swift, open stretches such as this one on the Tracker can take the boater on an uninterrupted sleigh ride for forty miles.*

NORTHWEST

Ringed entirely by mountain ranges, the rain-drenched Northwest claims a number of steep, glacial snowmelt rivers fed by vast glaciers and permanent snowfields. Most prominent—and most important to the paddler—is the Cascade range that runs from California due north into Canada, splitting the region into two unequal halves.

Most Northwest rivers, the Rogue excepted, have a boulder-strewn, uneven character. Low-volume streams twist down mountain slopes, dropping quickly over rocky rapids, then halting abruptly in dark pools. Rapids generally alternate between sheer vertical ledges, cascading sluices, and "garbage drops"—tight jumbles of various-sized boulders demanding a lot of zigzagging. The newcomer to this region will find currents surprisingly swift. Despite the plethora of rocks that inhibit water speed, unusually steep gradients keep all classes of river running quickly, if not continuously.

Greater in the Northwest than anywhere is the hazard of fallen trees. Endless stands of huge Ponderosa Pine cover the entire region east of the Cascades, while the larger western section is equally wooded with Douglas Fir. Both are extremely large, shallow-rooted trees, and tons of fresh timber fall across the paddler's path every spring.

Since both snowmelt and late autumn rains contribute to Northwestern streams, the paddling season is long, with many streams boatable all year round. Spring runoff starts in early March with rivers first cresting in late May. Then in late November and December heavy rains flood rivers again. In southern coastal sections that is the highest crest of the year.

The Northwest is not a region of extremes. It is less cold and rocky than the Northeast. And rivers lack the huge volume and length of the West. But for all levels of paddler, this region offers exciting white water and an aura of deep woods wilderness.

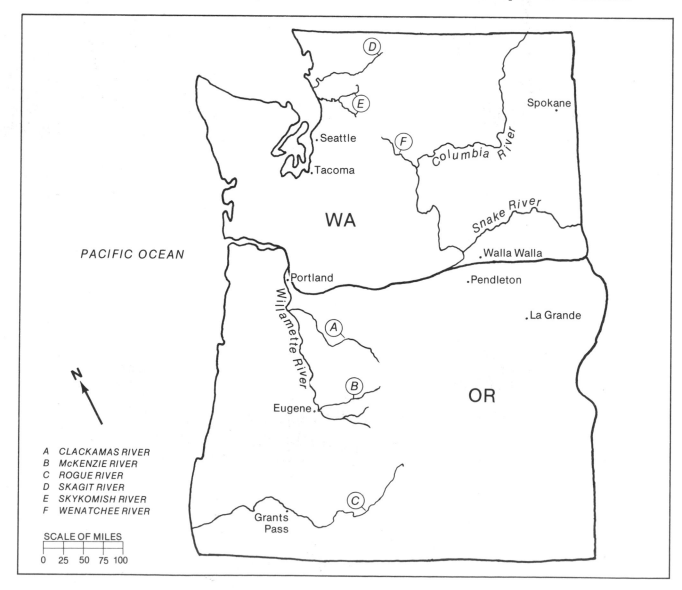

A CLACKAMAS RIVER
B McKENZIE RIVER
C ROGUE RIVER
D SKAGIT RIVER
E SKYKOMISH RIVER
F WENATCHEE RIVER

SCALE OF MILES

0   25   50   75 100

THOMPSON RIVER
The raft astern, glistening dark water, and a rocky, wooded shore all comprise a familiar whitewater scene in the Northwest.

Flathead River—North Fork

CLASS: 2

DESCRIPTION: Relatively wide, swift current; few obstructions; clear and cold.

STANDARD RUN: Put in at Flathead, B.C.; 21 mi. to Mud Creek, Mont., 7 mi. more to Polebridge and Bowman Creek Campsite.

LOCATION: River forms western boundary of Glacier Natl. Park, Mont.; put in right on Canadian border.

RUNNING SEASON: Mid-May through November.

Sometime in mid- to late May, the spring thaw breaks up the solid sheet of ice that has covered the Flathead since November and the clear, cold, glacial waters carry huge hunks of ice toward Flathead Lake. Soon after, the paddlers follow, wetsuited even in the first weeks of June. Despite summer weather the water temperature will remain below forty degrees until July.

From the canyon walls above, the Flathead looks like just another slow, meandering stream. But despite appearances, this river sweeps over its broad rock bed at eight miles per hour, with very few obstacles to interrupt. The pebbly banks occasionally constrict the current, causing a short series of standing waves. Eddies are far apart, found primarily on the inside of curves or behind one of the rare, car-size boulders.

More than a proving ground for Class-1+ paddlers, the Flathead provides the best possible view of Glacier National Park. Just twenty miles west of the Continental Divide and right below Kintla Glacier, dozens of little feeder streams pour clear mountain runoff and chalky glacier melt into the river.

Generally, the valley is open and lush, containing a treasure trove for the amateur geologist. Downstream from Kintla Glacier, the river twists through a 150-foot rock canyon that squeezes the current into some of the tightest and best rapids. Beyond this gorge riverside campsites are available at Mud Creek and Bowman Creek.

Although the Flathead wins no titles as Montana's most challenging whitewater, it remains some of the most popular. For the neophyte seeking to handle fast water or the cruiser wanting a different perspective on the northern Rockies, the Flathead offers an exciting blend of speed and scenery.

Skagit River

CLASS: 3

DESCRIPTION: Narrow, winding; large volume; large boulders, vertical drops and ledges; playable holes.

STANDARD RUN: Put in at Newhalem, Wash., off Rte. 20; 6 mi. to Bacon Creek campground, 75 mi. more of cruisable river into Puget Sound.

LOCATION: 2½ hrs. NE of Seattle, Wash., in North Cascades Natl. Park.

RUNNING SEASON: All year round.

Ten thousand years ago the last glacier stood quietly melting under the Pleistocene sun. As the ice sheet retreated slowly over Washington's northern Cascades, it left behind a mixture of glacial moraine, laying the course for the Skagit River. Today, the Skagit still flows through a bed of copper and other ores deposited by the glacier, which give the water a creamy turquoise color.

The Skagit's blue-green waters are presently fed by Ross Lake and controlled by three dams, which release a substantial flow almost every weekend of the year. The narrow banks fill quickly, and large haystacks run in long series, which provide bouncy, relatively rock-free sleigh rides. Most of the rapids are crisp, vertical drops followed by a curler and a long chute. Eddies are small but numerous, and they allow some breathing space in this continuous current.

Though the Skagit is generally an open river, there are a few, short boulder gardens that require technical maneuvering at a surprisingly high speed. The banks often close in, creating a sudden, accelerating chute that plunges you into a small patch of table-size rocks. Typical is S Bend, one of the Skagit's most renowned boat crunchers. As the name implies, the water rushes around two sharp bends, flowing over two rocky ledges and demanding a hard, fast zigzag.

The Skagit is a popular rafting river with nearly a dozen outfitters in the area. Access and egress are excellent with Route 20 running along this entire stretch of the river. Since the river is controlled by a dam, the occasional flood releases tend to wash away "sweepers"—shallow rooted trees that have fallen across the river and pin rafts and other less agile craft.

Note: The 75 miles below the Bacon Creek campground, though not whitewater, is some of the most geologically interesting, in the state. There are many sections where you can camp and cruise by day, including one in Mount Baker–Snoqualmie National Forest with an eagle refuge.

CHILCOTIN RIVER
Rafters (top) find it a bouncy ride through the haystacks of Railroad Rapids.

NORTH ALOUETTE RIVER
Dodging fallen trees (above) can be as tough as dodging rocks. And, if you miscalculate, there's no hull to protect you.

THOMPSON RIVER
(left) Warm weather, a sandy beach, and lunch give these river runners a chance to stretch their legs and drink in the glory of the Northwest.

Wenatchee River

CLASS: 2–3+

DESCRIPTION: Open, medium width; shoals and small rocks with swift, heavy-water canyon in middle.

STANDARD RUN: Put in at Scottish Falls bridge (N of Leavenworth, Wash., on Rte. 209; approx 7 mi. to Peshastin; or downstream put in off Rte. 209 near Plain, Wash.; 5½ mi. to Tumwater Campground.

LOCATION: 2 hrs. E of Seattle, Wash.; 17 mi. N of Wenatchee, Wash. (on eastern edge of Wenatchee Natl. Forest).

RUNNING SEASON: *Suggested* March through October. *Possible* all year round.

Some would-be whitewater boaters approach the sport with a dangerous sense of logic. They start by running a few rivers on their own "just to see if they like it." Then, after a month of caroming off rocks and swimming through rapids, they decide it is time to locate an expert mentor and get some training. All of which makes as much sense as trying out sky diving for a few weeks before joining a jump school. While the dangers of whitewater may not be so obvious to the beginner, they must not be ignored.

The Wenatchee is the kind of river the novice must especially watch out for. It makes an excellent training ground, but it can spell trouble for the beginner who is running alone. Most of the river between Scottish Falls and Peshastin is not difficult for any paddler with basic skills and some Class-1+-to-2 experience. Small boulders jumble together to make short, easily negotiated drops. The banks occasionally constrict, causing the boater to accelerate over a small rock garden or gravel shoal. At several places, particularly a group of pilings below Leavenworth, the paddler will find foot-high surfing waves, perfect for playing. But toward the end, the river narrows into Chumstick Canyon and suddenly increases to a Class-3+ challenge. The banks become steeper and narrower, and the bed changes from gravel to a rock shelf. As the current speeds up, the boulders become bigger and tighter, making higher drops. In low water it is a long technical rock garden, demanding split-second reflexes. At higher levels, the rocks submerge, making a minefield of holes. If you have a competent expert to lead the way, this section is a pleasant and playable challenge for the new intermediate. If you are a neophyte alone on the river, unaware that this tougher section exists, you will be over your head—literally.

The Wenatchee's banks hold an unusual amount of hardwoods mingled with the predominant Ponderosa pine. These deciduous trees make a lovely fall foliage trip, particularly through the upper section from Plain to Tumwater Campground.

Clackamas River

CLASS: 1–2+

DESCRIPTION: Shallow; narrow to medium width shoals and some ledgy drops alternate with long flat; many bends.

STANDARD RUN: Put in at McIver Park near Estacada, Ore.; 21 long mi. to take-out just outside Gladstone.

LOCATION: 30 min. SE of Portland, Ore., via Rte. 224.

RUNNING SEASON: *Possible* all year round, even sometimes in midwinter. *Suggested* late April through July.

No matter how tough you are, starting a new sport, particularly one like whitewater canoeing, knots the gut and gives it butterflies. Both boat and situation feel totally out of control. But you've got to battle it out these first few weekends if you're ever going to have any fun in the sport, and the Clackamas is an ideal river on which to start. Much of the run flows swiftly, giving the uncertain neophyte the feel of a solid current underneath his boat. Most of the rapids are small, ledge-type drops where the paddler lines up the boat, hits the slot, and gets carried down a fast tongue of water with eddies on either side and perhaps some easy rock dodging. In addition, there are many riffles from shoals in the wider channels, demanding that the boater pick his course a long way in advance and aim for the deepest section of the river.

Though the Clackamas does not boast very long rapids, below each of the short drops a swift moving pool runs for several hundred yards. Instead of having to paddle long stretches of flat water to get to one small, quick chute, the boater has the sense of being on a continuously rushing river.

In those flat, open sections, the boater can lay down his paddle and see, towering above the Douglas fir that line the river, the snowcapped peak of Mount Hood just thirty miles away. At the foot of Oregon's highest peak move ancient glaciers that occasionally can be glimpsed from the canoe and whose milky melt continually feeds the river. The beauty of this tree-lined stream, along with the forgiving if challenging character of its rapids, makes the Clackamas an excellent learners' river: a possible one-day trip, but a more leisurely trip if completed in two days.

PLAYING THE RIVER AND OTHER PASTIMES
*Wave surfing : The paddlers of this old 3-holer
C-2 are powering upstream so they can ferry back and
forth on the curler (white wave in the foreground) and
not be swept downstream.*

Skykomish River

CLASS: 3–4

DESCRIPTION: Wide and winding; relatively heavy volume; many haystacks; medium length boulder patches with varying-size rocks.

STANDARD RUN: Put in below Sunset Falls at Index, Wash.; 7 mi. to take-out at Gold Bar bridge.

LOCATION: 30 min. NE of Seattle along Rte. 2.

RUNNING SEASON: Possible all year; river crests in December, also high in March and April.

The Skykomish is the only river included in Washington's Wild and Scenic Rivers Bill. This means that within an hour of the state's largest city flows a clean river fed by snowfields and mountain runoff that will be forever protected against commercial development.

The Skykomish runs off the west side of the Pacific Cascade Ridge, cutting a narrow canyonlike valley as it goes. It plunges first over Eagle Falls, then sixty-five feet over Sunset Falls into a cold five-acre pool. It is on this dark, still pool, just below the picturesque Sunset Falls, that the boater puts in for seven miles of heavy, technical whitewater.

For the first three miles, the river remains in its tight canyon flowing through constricted banks over a litter of varying-size boulders. These boulders split the river into several narrow channels and create steep, rock-strewn cascades that natives call garbage drops. Gravel shoals jut out from the side and combine with boulders to form a natural slalom course.

After the first three miles and the confluence with the North Fork, the river flattens out a little but adds more pool-and-drop rapids. Just downstream from the take-out, the closed boater can continue through an expert-only section called Boulder Drop. For a mile and a half the river pitches steeply over a very tight patch of truck-size boulders that are known boat crunchers. If you are wondering whether or not to run this Class-4-to-5 stretch, remember that the water remains close to forty degrees Fahrenheit all year; your chances of a very cold dunking are excellent.

Water level means everything on the Skykomish. Like most of Washington's coastal rivers it reaches high crest during the runoff in April and again in December during the winter rains. At these times the Skykomish runs up to 3,000 cfs. The rest of the year, melt from vast nearby snowfields maintains a constant flow of 1,000 cfs.

McKenzie River

CLASS: 3–4

DESCRIPTION: Narrow, winding, steady drop; continuous, fast current; heavy water.

STANDARD RUN: Put in upstream of McKenzie Bridge, Ore., on Rte. 126; 10 mi. to McKenzie Bridge take-out; 25 more mi. to Leaburg, Ore.

LOCATION: 3 hrs. SE of Portland, Ore. Just S of Mt. Washington Wilderness in Deschutes Natl. Forest.

RUNNING SEASON: Possible all year round. Suggested mid-February to October. Crests in late May to early June.

"If you have to put your chains on, fergit it" goes a Northwest boater's proverb. When the snows get so deep that you have to plow your way to the put-in, you are better off spending the weekend skiing. This advice puts paddlers out on the McKenzie just about every weekend of the year, long after New Englanders of comparable latitude have yielded to the cold.

The McKenzie is a modest-sized stream with a deceptive amount of power. A current of 1500 cubic feet per second flows swiftly and at a constant pitch over a bed of small rocks that create large haystacks. These endless series of standing waves, particularly on the lower section, form a delightful, wild sleigh ride.

Playing on a river this swift is catch-as-catch-can. You can wave surf to your heart's content. Backwards, sideways, any way you can drop into the deep notch between haystacks twenty feet apart.

The McKenzie also boasts several large, boulder-filled rapids with playable souseholes. Martin Rapids, a nearly vertical cascade, drops almost seven feet and ends in a hydraulic. At Brown's Hole, just below the McKenzie Bridge put-in, the river narrows to one-third its normal width and chutes over rocks into a curler as wide as the river. This large sousehole has beaten many excellent boaters.

Basically, the McKenzie is an exciting, scenic river where you can spend all day surfing two miles of waves or, in the same time, cruising the twenty-five miles to Leaburg. But there is one danger even for experienced boaters. The river is lined with Douglas fir, a shallow-rooted tree that has a great tendency to fall across rivers. The McKenzie winds frequently, creating many blind curves to hide the fallen trees. But if you have a wary bowman, the McKenzie makes an excellent weekend paddle.

Rogue River

CLASS: 3–4

DESCRIPTION: Medium width, winding; submerged boulders, holes; some long rock gardens alternating with long stretches of flat water.

STANDARD RUN: Put in at Grave Creek, Ore.; 35 mi. to Foster Bar.

LOCATION: 2½ hrs. south of Eugene, Ore. (in Siskiyou Natl. Forest).

RUNNING SEASON: All year round; 750–2,000 cfs in low, summer levels, crest in early spring and December (floods up to 40,000 cfs).

The Rogue is a river that has it all. Long continuous sleigh rides through high standing waves, fast and tight boulder gardens demanding split-second rock dodging, steep vertical drops, and discouragingly long sections of flat water all make up the Rogue's varied and unique character. Thus, the paddler devoting two or three days to these thirty-five miles confronts every type of river obstacle from waterfalls to "tubers."

Three miles below the Grave Creek put-in, the Rogue plunges over Rainie Falls, a high, vertical drop into a hydraulic that could hold a freight train. This Class-5-to-6 waterfall should be portaged by all but a few of the ultrabuoyant 18-foot rafts.

Aside from Rainie Falls, the Rogue runs pool-drop–pool with the long sections of flat water broken by varied rock gardens and Class-3 sluices. The narrow river cuts a deep channel through a V-shaped canyon, flowing 750–2,000 cubic feet per second in summer—the most popular running time. The winding canyon walls, ranging from fifteen- to a hundred-feet high, are well scoured by flooding in early spring and again in December. (Natives tell of the "Christmas of '64 flood," when torrential rains caused the Rogue to swell over its banks with a raging current of 200,000 cfs.)

Due to their length and unforgiving nature, two long rapids on the Rogue confront the paddler with a solid Class-4 challenge. Mule Creek Canyon runs for a continuous mile over submerged boulders. The holes are strong and the side eddies are replaced by mushrooming boilers, making rescue virtually impossible. If you dump at the top of this one, you swim for a mile. Lodge owners note that no one wearing a life jacket has ever died on this swim. But for several paddlers who were not, it was a different story. Shortly below Mule Creek lies Blossom Bar, a congested drop full of jagged rocks just waiting to grab the paddler who cuts a little too close. It was caused by motorboaters who tried unsuccessfully to dynamite a pathway upstream.

Below Blossom Bar the paddler is assaulted by the roar of jetsleds—a form of floating snowmobile that can be a real hazard. Most of the commercial rafters run from June to Labor Day, and the powerboat fishermen, seeking steelhead salmon, come mostly in September and October. For the rest of the year the Rogue is relatively open.

Note: Paddlers can camp anywhere along the river. To avoid crowding, park rangers will suggest sites. Also three overnight lodges along the thirty-five-mile run welcome paddlers. (Reservations must be made well in advance because the lodges fill quickly.)

SKYKOMISH RIVER
This is the reason spray skirts were invented.

CALIFORNIA

Most of California's white water is contained in the Central Valley river system. Running off the steep western slopes of the Sierra and Cascade ranges, this network of more or less parallel rivers cuts a westward path through the heart of the state, across the 450-mile wide valley toward the Pacific Ocean. Much of the other California white water flows from the coastal ranges in the North.

The variety of California rivers is infinite. Generally, the Sierra and rivers running out of the Sierras or Cascades are steep, winding, and open. Boulders of all sizes exist, but the powerful, continuous currents call for more heavy-water skills than rock dodging. Heavy rapids are due more to the entrance of a side tributary than to piles of talus or glacial boulders, though rocks and rock gardens become more prevalent at the end of the season. The northern Coastal range rivers generally claim lesser gradients with rapids formed by shoal-constricted banks with some technical rock piles.

April through September are the prime paddling months, with free-flowing rivers cresting in early May. Unfortunately, irrigation and power needs have engendered a statewide dam system, controlling most major rivers and obliterating some others. As a small compensation, California is one of the few states where the recreational planning includes whitewater paddling as a major consideration, and state planners work with local clubs to develop easy access roads and convenient water releases.

Rafting is everywhere in California, and commercial outfitters offer guided trips or just equipment on most rivers. Kayaks are the prominent whitewater boat, while open canoes are used primarily by campers. The C-1 is seldom seen except at slalom races.

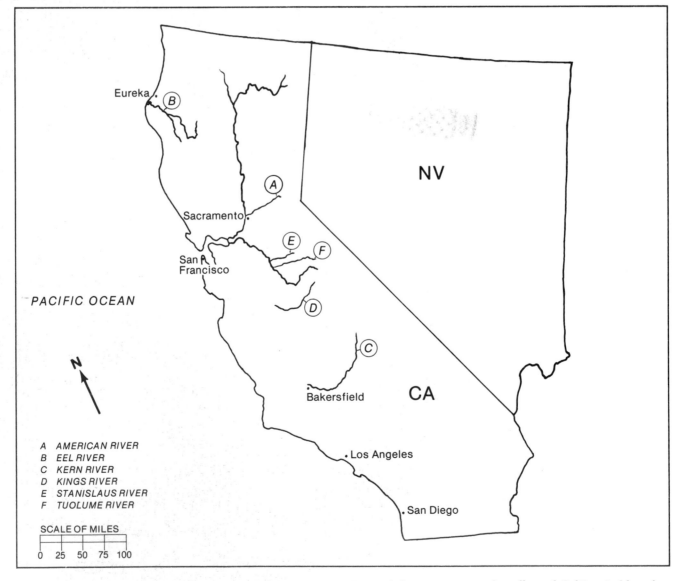

A   AMERICAN RIVER
B   EEL RIVER
C   KERN RIVER
D   KINGS RIVER
E   STANISLAUS RIVER
F   TUOLUME RIVER

SCALE OF MILES

0   25   50   75   100

Beneath bare, craggy rock walls and California blue sky (opposite), a paddler wends his way through a messy rock garden. An inflatable K-1 is the first step up from a raft toward real kayaking.

American River

CLASS: *South Fork—3 + -4. Main Fork—2*
DESCRIPTION: *South Fork*—Broad; continuous, swift current; mostly boulder fields; some constricted chutes. *Main Fork*—Broad, slow meandering current; some small haystacks, much flat.
STANDARD RUN: *South Fork*—Put in just above Chilly Bar, Calif.; via dirt road off Rte. 193; 6 mi. to Sutter's Mill (just outside Coloma). (The Gorge and other short sections are runnable to Folsom Lake depending on water level.) *Main Fork*—Put in at Sailor Bar NE of Sacramento, Calif.; 12 mi. to Arden Rapids by Greenbelt Pkwy. bike trail—just upstream of confluence with Sacramento R. and town center.
LOCATION: *South Fork*—1 hr. NE of Sacramento, Calif. *Main Fork*—Western section of Sacramento, Calif.
RUNNING SEASON: March through November, depending on releases.

In January 1848 James Wilson Marshall rode from the South Fork of the American River into the small settlement of Sacramento, poured out a sackful of nuggets that announced to the world that "they found gold at Sutter's Mill." Within a year thousands of hungry fortune hunters flooded into California, setting up sluice boxes on the American and many other then-free-flowing rivers.

Today, the historic Sutter's Mill marks the take-out of one of California's more popular and interesting runs. If you've got the experience and a good, solid roll, the South Fork of the American can be a delightful, if tricky, challenge. The current flows swiftly and fairly continuously over a broad and sometimes sharply winding riverbed. Varying-size boulders frequently jumble together, forming intermediate drops. Even the local experts admit that this stream's a real stinker to read. Quarter-mile Rapids, soon after the put-in, forms a chute against the steep side of the mountain. But it pitches off so sharply that you can backender if you don't keep chugging. S Turn looks like a tough, but manageable zigzag between boulder-pile ledges. But hiding between the zig and the zag, like a troll under a bridge, is a surprise sousehole, just made for biting off hot-doggers. If Sutter's Mill and the ghosts of the Gold Rush entice you, but dropping your K-1 into a Class-4-keeper doesn't, you can make this scenic run by commerical or private raft. The South Fork runs out of the Sierra foothills with usually gently sloping banks, covered with California oak, pine, and scrub brush. In addition, an obstacle unique to this stream is the weekend prospector running his small wooden sluice gate, searching for gold. The spirit of the Forty-niners still survives.

Main Fork

If you're lucky enough to live in Sacramento, or if you're just passing through, sheer convenience demands you give the American's whitewater a whirl. Find yourself a mentor, get outfitted at the local livery (see p.124), and put in from Sailor Bar by the Greenbelt Parkway bike trail. It is an ideal trip for those who seek a small taste of whitewater but who don't want to bite off more than they can chew.

In these last few miles before it empties into the Sacramento River, the American makes a slow, but surprisingly forceful meander over a medium-width rock and clay bed. Arden Rapids at the take-out and many of the standing waves are formed by these large rough lumps of clay—a little easier on your boat than jagged granite.

But the real, and virtually only, novice eater is San Juan Rapids. These are a long series of standing waves followed by a clay, washboardlike chute, with a beautiful beginners' surfing wave at the end. It makes a safe, forgiving play spot where the starting paddler can get the feel of water current.

Unlike most urban rivers, paddling on the American is thoroughly enjoyable. Constant local effort has kept the river unpolluted. The banks are just high enough to cut off that mass-civilization view and the woodsy Greenbelt Parkway bike trail follows the entire run.

TOM JOHNSON
(opposite) *The old California pro zigzags his kayak from chute* (in background) *to drop* (in foreground).

Stanislaus River

CLASS: *Camp Nine—3 + –4. Parrots Ferry—2*

DESCRIPTION: *Camp Nine*—Strong, medium-width current; short rocky rapids; high haystacks, varying-length pools. *Parrots Ferry*—Smaller version of Camp Nine run; short, open rapids; bouncy waves; long flat.

STANDARD RUN: Camp Nine below dam, put in from road between Vallecito and Columbia, Calif.; 9 mi. to take-out at Parrots Ferry, 9 mi. more to Melones campground.

LOCATION: 2 hrs SE of Sacramento, Calif.

RUNNING SEASON: April through November, depending on dam-controlled water releases.

The Upper Stanislaus is the river for a whitewater workout. Look on this stretch for that young hotshot training to tear up next spring's slalom courses. You'll see him spinning his paddle in a hole near Swinging Bridge Rapids or working the gates of the Camp Nine slalom course, which hang all year round at the put-in.

Even if you're not next year's champ but just an experienced paddler looking for some hotdogging, this is a perfectly delightful run. Large glacier-carved, granite boulders form narrow, steep chutes with four- and five-foot haystacks and wide side eddies—excellent for surfing. Many of the rocks at every level are submerged, making broad holes for spinning and popping enders.

Don't be deceived—the Stanislaus does take substantial skill. Many of the rapids, though short, are quite technical, demanding quick reflexes. But for those who have the ability, it's a trip to experiment on: The holes are seldom keepers, and you never have to swim very far to the next pool.

Even the most myopic of whitewater athletes cannot run the Stanislaus without some appreciation of its magnificient beauty. Groves of California oak (along with some poison oak) grow right down to the edge of the water. Nine-hundred-foot cliffs, striated with up-edged limestone veins, and bearded with stalactites form a one-sided gorge. House-size boulders create calm little swimming eddies and pools. Nearly forty thousand people float the Stanislaus annually, almost double the numbers that crowd the Grand Canyon. With this much beauty and exhilarating water, it's not difficult to see why.

Parrots Ferry

The lower run is basically a milder version of the Camp Nine section. The river opens up on its way to the Melones Reservoir, and the current becomes less constricted and a little slower. The rapids consist primarily of dodging a rock or two at the top, then following the chute down into the pool below.

The Class-2 paddler who isn't too picky about chugging through some long flat stretches will be rewarded with some bouncy sleigh rides and much the same awesome scenery found on the upper run. If you have the weekend, camp at the Melones campground by the take-out. The fishing is superlative, the view inspiring, and—with the exception of midsummer—the crowds are not quite overwhelming.

Eel River

CLASS: 2+ to 3
DESCRIPTION: Medium width; fair current; many boulders causing channels of varying widths.
STANDARD RUN: Put in at town of Hearst, Calif.; 18 mi. to Outlet Creek.
STANDARD RUN: Put in at Alderpoint, Calif.; 25 mi. to McCann bridge.
LOCATION: 2½ hrs. N of San Francisco, Calif.
RUNNING SEASON: March through May.

It happens to boaters, especially the fanatics. Cruisers or racers, we rivet our attention so intensely on this rapid or that hole, on sharpening up that pry, that we ignore the whole beauty of the whitewater experience. We myopically reduce paddling to a series of bouncy jolts that challenge our athletic prowess. If that grim pursuit of skill is all you're getting out of canoeing, the Eel is an excellent river to pull you out of that rut.

The Eel is a beautiful, semiwilderness stream where steep pine slopes, herds of deer, slowly spiraling hawks, and even an occasional brown bear are as much a part of your weekend as the challenge of water. Much of the 18 miles to Outlet Creek consists of long, not overly difficult rock gardens and riffly gravel bars, alternating with short-to-medium flat stretches. But the real spice of this river is the frequent, short-but-sweet rapids where large, rugged boulders form swift, multitongued chutes with ample side eddies. Some of the currents are deceptively tricky, particularly in Rock Section, yet most are very playable with long curlers and surfing waves.

The clear, cold waters of the Eel thaw a little earlier than most, which gives it an earlier, colder running season. This need for wetsuits may make it less inviting to some, but those willing to go a little further north, a little earlier in the season, will be rewarded with a weekend of solitude and scenic beauty.

Tuolumne River

CLASS: 4+ –6 (closed boat)
DESCRIPTION: Heavy, swift, powerful current; huge boulders, deep drops, and holes.
STANDARD RUN: Put in right off Rte. 120 ¾ mi. after W border of Yosemite Park, Calif.; 18 mi. along Rte. 120 to take-out—past Harden Flat, Calif.
LOCATION: 5 hrs. E of San Francisco, Calif.; just W of Yosemite Natl. Park.
RUNNING SEASON: April to July; end of May suggested for safety.

It's big, it's hairy, and it can eat you alive. If there's any other river in the state of California that gives you the slightest pause, stay away from the Tuolumne. There are rare occasions when the water drops to an experienced-intermediate level. But most of the time it rages somewhere between expert level and unrunnable, and it takes all your paddling skill to tell the difference.

Down in a three-quarter-mile deep canyon the Tuolumne's current rampages through vertical granite walls and endless jumbles of house-size boulders. The rapids thus created are narrow, twisting channels that drop you off the edge of nowhere into huge, foaming hydraulics. Often you'll plunge into a churning sinkhole, disappearing completely, and, if you're lucky, you'll get spit out into a tight field of smaller boulders.

If the riverwide keeper holes and ten-feet high haystacks don't make you fidget just a little, there is an additional danger: You're trapped. After about the first mile you are committed to the trip. Hiking out would demand rope and pitons.

But aside from being dangerous, the Tuolumne Canyon houses some of the state's most spectacular landscape. Massive, glacier-etched cliffs towering overhead, ancient petroglyphs marking the dwellings of the first Americans, broad vistas of rushing water, placid inlets loaded with rainbow trout—all can be viewed safely on a commercially guided raft trip. If possible, make the Tuolumne a weekend expedition and camp on the floor of the canyon. This river is the ultimate in beauty and challenge; paddle it if you can, but if you can't, set macho aside and raft it. It is a wilderness experience rarely equalled in any region.

BOILING WATER

(above) *He's not over yet. A kayakist playing in a hole braces himself with his blade.* (center) *Another kayakist drives into a hole for a pop-up. The falling water has already pushed his bow under slightly and lifted his stern. Olympic paddler Russ Nichols watches in the background.* (below) *Rafters, their load well distributed, bounce through a tongue.*

Kings River

CLASS: *Upper Kings—4. Lower Kings—2.*

DESCRIPTION: *Upper Kings*—Medium width; fast, steep rapids followed by short pools; many tricky boulder fields. *Lower Kings*—Somewhat wider than the Upper Kings; shoaly drops and quick turns in average current; long flat.

STANDARD RUN: *Upper Kings*—Put in at Garnet Dike in Sierra Natl. Forest, Calif.; 9 mi. to Kirsh Flat. *Lower Kings*—Put in at bridge below Pine Flat Dam (above Piedra, Calif.); 21 mi. to Centerville (put in at dam and run first 10 mi. for 1-day trip).

LOCATION: *Upper Kings*—2½ hrs. E of Fresno, Calif. *Lower Kings*—1½ hrs. E of Fresno, Calif.

RUNNING SEASON: *Upper Kings*—April through June. *Lower Kings*—Dam-controlled, varying releases, run all year; check local clubs for info.

"Oh Gawd, here it comes: Banzai!" You've heard this rapid talked up for seasons: the huge haystacks, the keepers, the steep pitch-off. And it would have to be right near the put-in. Your gut clenches to a golf-ball and makes you wish you were with the smart ones, portaging this stretch. "Well, here it goes." You churn your blade for all your worth, certain that you are dropping off the edge of the earth. Then about a year and a half through the rapid, you suddenly gain some perspective. "Yes, all those stories were true: the haystacks really are enormous, those two holes really could hold me. But I can miss 'em. I've got the skill, and I can even relax—just a little." Then all too soon you flush into a pool and draw into a side eddy, sitting there with the smug elation that comes from conquering a legend.

For the experienced intermediate, the **Upper Kings** is a goal to shoot for, with a high fear factor. A strong current slams around some sharp S turns creating high standing waves. Truck-size boulders sprinkle the river, easy to avoid but causing swift, flumelike channels. For the most part, the boulder fields are easy to maneuver, but high haystacks and large rocks can make vision difficult.

The road follows the river from about five hundred feet above as it winds through Sierra National Forest. Oak and pine line the shores giving a nice blend of forest and canyon. Despite its beauty, the Upper Kings can be a dangerous river. Like so many rivers in this region, snowmelt means everything and rapids like Gravel Pit, Ranch, or Kirsch Flat can become Class 5 or even unrunnable in early spring. Don't even put in on this one without some experts in the party and a previous knowledge of the water level.

If you're an open boater who likes a full weekend of canoe camping but wants more whitewater and less company than is possible with the overboated Russian River, try the twenty-one miles below Pine Flat Dam. The reservoir behind the dam irrigates most of the farmland in California's huge Central Valley, and thus the water flow is totally controlled by dam release. Generally this makes a long season; you can be running the **Lower Kings** in midsummer, when everything else is dry.

Most of this medium-width river is open and somewhat shallow, making rocks easy to read and avoid. But there are several drops that frequently occur around tight, constricted corners, which can greet the unwary with a surprisingly tight pass or slam against the bank. There are two short but mandatory portages throughout the run. The first, Alta Wier, has a warning sign and points to a portage route. The second is a small dam approximately five miles from the take-out.

If you want a day trip, put in at the Pine Flat Dam and run down about ten miles. This includes most of the best rapids, and since the road follows the river all the way, you can spot a car anywhere. But wherever you run, don't mistake this for a totally novice river. It can be tricky and should not be run without someone who's been through it all before.

FEATHER RIVER
(opposite top) *Once one of the state's most popular and challenging rivers, it now stands placid, robbed of its white water by a series of dams and conduits.*
(opposite bottom) *Popular in regions with more open rivers, inflatables such as this are less maneuverable than a solid kayak but are more forgiving and demand less skill.*

Kern River

CLASS: *Kernville—2+-4. Hart Park—1-2*

DESCRIPTION: *Kernville*—Broad bed; short steep technical rapids followed by short pools; two slalom sites en route. *Hart Park*—Continuous shallow current, spiced with shoals and riffles; popular for beginners.

STANDARD RUN: *Kernville*—Put in by Cable Put-in (5 mi. upriver along northward road); 5 mi. to Kernville, Calif., 6 mi. more to Lake Isabella. *Hart Park*—Put in at west end of Hart Park in Bakersfield, Calif.; 1½ mi. toward Bakersfield center (local roads follow).

LOCATION: *Kernville*—2 hrs. N of Los Angeles, Calif. *Hart Park*—1½ hrs. N of Los Angeles, Calif.

RUNNING SEASON: *Kernville*—April through June; other times shallow but possible. *Hart Park*—April through September; dam controlled.

"When I die," said one Ohio paddler, "I'm going to go to Kernville and have the Kern River flow right through my backyard." To most travel-weary paddlers, the prospect of living smack dab in the middle of forty miles of Class-2-to-4 whitewater and having two year-round slalom courses within three miles of home must be pretty darn close to heaven. To make it all a little more perfect, the best eleven miles of the run starts five miles from your house, and a road follows the entire stretch.

Immediately after you put in at Cable Put-in, the Camp Three rapids grab you. Then for the first five miles it's pool and plunge with plenty of wide stoppers that take a lot of churning to punch through. These curlers are generally not dangerous but are easy to roll in if you slow your stroke rate. The most dangerous rapid is a soup strainer called Wall, where the current slams against a rock-studded dirt cliff that shoots you down a fast cascade into a sharp sousehole just made for unintentional back-enders.

At two slalom courses—Lazy River Rapids and three miles downstream at Kernville's Riverside Park—boaters struggle to use the current and maneuver their way through narrow gates—several pairs of poles overhanging the river. The course in Kernville is particularly fascinating because boulders were planted by the Army Corps of Engineers and local paddling enthusiasts to reshape this two-hundred-yard section of river. Working the gates on this course for one afternoon will do more for your paddling ability than five weekend cruises.

Below Kernville the stream broadens considerably and opens up, making those wide stoppers easier to avoid. The water level often becomes scratchy in this stretch toward summer. But whatever the level, the idea of jumping in your car and making a quick, after-dinner run, is something paddlers dream about every time they make that five-hour haul to the nearest water.

You don't launch on a thirty-mile weekend expedition to discover if you like whitewater any more than you'd swallow a whole hog to find out whether you like ham. Instead, spend an afternoon taking one or two runs on the mile-and-a-half section of the Kern that flows through Hart Park.

This pleasant little section of Class 1 and 2 gives a varied sample of what it's like to handle river current. This broad, shallow run of the Kern has everything from riffles to shoals to even a little minicurler if the water level's right. It is a popular starter river for beginners and not only because of its length; since it is dam controlled, you can take the plunge in midsummer, a more comfortable season.

A final warning: Do not start off on whitewater, on the Kern or anywhere, without a mentor. It is stupid and unsafe. And even if you do survive, the odds of your learning something are very small.

The point of it all . . . White Water is Fun!

Reading the River

Half the art of paddling is knowing where to go and what to avoid. And though at first glance the river may appear a fathomless mass of rocks and boiling white, water does not flow haphazardly. There *are* patterns and they are discernible from the boat.

Reading these patterns is a skill that you never stop learning. For the experienced paddler it is almost instinctive, but with surprisingly little study the neophyte can learn to spot some basic signs and elements of current that will help him make some sense out of the river.

How to Look

River running is primarily a matter of following the river and avoiding the obstacles in its path. So in studying a rapid, don't just stare at the rocks. Follow a piece of water with your eyes. Look where the water is flowing above the rapid, where it piles up within it, and where it comes out at the bottom. Below are some predictable water patterns that apply to all levels and sizes of rivers.

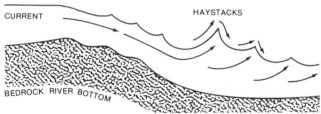

Haystacks Standing waves that are rounded or pointed caused by a) increased incline or b) constriction of the current, for example by narrow banks. These regular, stationary hills of water indicate the line of unobstructed current. Often a good route to follow depends on wave height and ferocity. (Haystacks can be 2-inch riffles, or 10-foot waves.) *Hint:* The irregular-looking wave in a line of haystacks is probably a hidden rock.

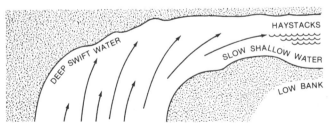

Current Flow Given its head, a river naturally flows in a straight line until the banks force it to bend or turn. A river runs neither willingly nor evenly between its confines, but caroms off them. When the banks curve sharply, the water rushes on straight ahead, slamming into and hugging the outside bank. Water piles up, forming haystacks on this outside turn, while the inside water runs shallower and slower. *Hint:* If the river is low, head to the outside for maximum depth. If it's heavy and a little scary, head for the slower inside current.

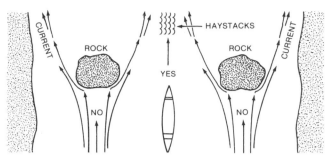

Obstacles With a few exceptions (like a downed tree), anything that blocks your path also obstructs the current. If you must go around it, so must the water. When a rock is above the surface, this is obvious: The current piles against the rock's upstream edge, then splits into two lines of current on either side. When an obstacle is submerged, the boater can still read these divergent current lines. Trace these lines to where they join. If they come together *upstream* and form a V, avoid the apex and go around it: There's a rock. *Hint:* if you see the lines joining *downstream* in an inverted V, the rocks are on either side and you can head for that slot.

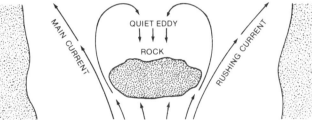

The Eddy As the current slams into an obstruction and current lines diverge downstream, a quiet space—an eddy—is formed immediately below the obstacle. Water curls around the rock and floods into this quiet spot below. Here the water is relatively still, or even flowing slightly in reverse—upstream toward the rock. It's an excellent spot to rest mid-river without drifting.

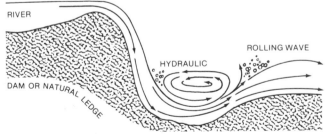

Hydraulic (also a *hole, curler,* or *roller*) Generally found at the base of a dam, natural ledge, or some steep drop. Water pours over an obstacle (seen or unseen), plunges down, and curls back on itself, forming a stationary rolling wave. Here the water, actually rolling upstream, is often strong enough to stop and hold a boat, with or without the paddler's consent. Depending on their size, hydraulics are places for the experienced to play—and novices to avoid.

Whitewater Safety—the Skill of Survival

Whitewater boating is dangerous. Every year people are killed on rivers, not necessarily because they are stupid or ill-equipped but because they lack definite survival skills. Being safe on a river demands more than a cautious state of mind. It involves mastering a particular body of technique—beyond good boat handling and water reading. Below are listed some of these basic techniques and other general rules.

Choosing a Club

Romantic photos and appealing adventure tales usually lure neophytes into the sport, where they wallow along, untrained and unsupported. Any club is better than none, but finding the right one usually takes time. Some clubs are little more than a list of phone numbers. While this may be O.K. for the experienced river runner, the beginner needs more. If you're just starting, try to find a club with a solid instruction program, a good schedule of beginning rivers, and responsible leaders who are willing to teach the kind of paddling you want. A good club teaches more than boating skills. It instills a knowledge of rescue, proper equipment, and first aid.

Group Running

Running any level of white water alone is suicidal. In groups of 2 to 6 boats use the "buddy system," with teams of two keeping an eye on each other. In groups of 7 to 12 boats, the leader should appoint a front admiral and a sweep boat with all other boats staying in between. For groups of more than 12 boats, break into two groups, each with a front admiral and sweep boat. Each boater is responsible for wearing a helmet and life jacket, carrying a spare paddle and a waterproof change of clothes, or wearing a wetsuit. And be sure to have good solid equipment. The group leader should make sure there is at least one full first-aid kit and one throw rope (100 to 200 feet) for every six boats.

Rescue

Unless you know how to rescue yourself, you shouldn't be on the river. Each paddler must know the techniques for getting himself safely ashore; how to flush through heavy water with feet up to avoid leg trapping; how to fend off rocks; and how to keep upstream of your own boat. Knowledge of boat rescue is only slightly less vital.

First Aid

Ideally, every paddler should have a basic knowledge of first aid. Practically, at least two people in the party must. Icy cold waters cause hypothermia—the inability of the body to maintain its own heat—a primary hazard of paddling. Each paddler should be aware of the signs: blue nails and lips, uncontrolled shivering, confused mind and speech. And somewhere in the group should be the knowledge and equipment to rewarm a victim.

Should I Run This Stretch?

Fear and courage are terrible criteria. So is peer pressure. Deciding whether to run demands judgment. Your best bet is to find a mentor—a solid, experienced paddler who has run the river before and whose opinion you trust and ask him:

- What class of river is it at *this water level?* (see the A.C.A. River Rating Classification at the end of the glossary)
- What river does it compare to that we've run before?
- Can I scout and portage the hairy parts easily?
- Is a roll mandatory?
- What should I watch for?
  Then ask yourself:
- What is the strength of this group?
- Are they skilled *and willing* in rescue situations?
- Are my ability, muscles, spirit, and equipment up to this river? *Don't lie.*

Whitewater river running involves risk. But if the risk is uncalculated, then it is foolish and can easily be tragic.

Competition

While canoe and kayak have historically been means of outdoor transportation, whitewater paddling today is basically a sport. Competition, an artificial means of testing one's ability on a river, is a natural outgrowth.

Two kinds of whitewater races are prevalent.

Wildwater racing is simply a timed run straight down river. Start and finish are determined more by tradition than exact mileage. Decked boats usually run a 5 to 8 mile course, while open boaters run from 5 to 20 miles. Boats have been developed specifically for wildwater racing that are sleeker, faster, and a little less maneuverable than regular cruising boats.

Slalom racing is a way of making a tough stream tougher. It demands from a paddler more precision and quicker reflexes and slightly less raw power than a wildwater race. The competitors race over a short course (usually ⅓ to ¼ mi.) maneuvering body and boat through a series of numbered "gates." These gates consist of a red and a green pole hung over the water just a bit farther apart than your boat's width. Depending on the arrangement of the poles and various gate signs, the racer must paddle between each set of poles, in order, facing either backwards, forwards, from upstream or downstream.

The action is fast paced and exhausting. Good paddlers spend about 3 minutes running 30 gates packed into a 400 yard race course. But you cannot sacrifice precision for speed. The slightest error—touching a pole with body, boat or

IT'S A WRAP . . .
(opposite) *The price you pay for misjudging. Although this canoe might seem demolished, many boats like this have been salvaged and made new again. Notice the lines running out to the canoe that will pull it into shore. Keep this picture in mind when you feel like running a rapid you know you can't handle yet.*

blade—adds penalty seconds to your time. Since your final score is the number of seconds taken to run the course, plus the penalty seconds, the race goes to the swiftest *and* the sharpest.

Most races are sponsored by whitewater clubs and are strictly for amateur paddlers. Devoted racers travel hundreds of miles every weekend following the racing circuit, leading first to the Nationals and then to the World Championships.

Today, whitewater paddling is no longer a small, intimate sport. At the top competition is intense, and to come even close to the top demands a grueling schedule of daily training, long weekend drives, and hours spent repairing equipment. But if you don't aspire to this rarified atmosphere, do not be put off by the struggle of the titans. *There's a place in racing for everybody.* Most races are now divided into ability-classes, so the hardened cruiser who has never raced or the anxious neophyte can compete among his peers and have a fun, educational experience.

But a race is more than competition. For spectators, beginners, and even experts it is a weekend-paddling school where you can discover new techniques, sharpen old skills, and work. After competing, each paddler serves as a gate judge—an excellent chance to observe top boaters, see which way they go, and how they utilize the current to get there.

At night, the river bank transforms itself into a paddler's hobo jungle. Here, amid the wet clothes and fiberglass, the beginner can get all the latest paddling news—about new equipment, what rivers are running next weekend, where to find your kind of paddling club or a used boat, and building or repair techniques—all seasoned with some unbelieveable boasts and outright lies. The atmosphere is friendly and warm; there exists no better place to learn every aspect of whitewater boating.

(below, left and right) *The thrill of slalom competition excites the onlookers as well as the competitors.*

Clubs

Any book's club list must necessarily be incomplete and too quickly out of date. The most up-to-date list is in the current issue of *American Whitewater Magazine.*

NATIONAL ORGANIZATIONS

American Canoe Association (A.C.A.)
4260 East Evans Ave.
Denver, Colo. 80222

American Whitewater Affiliation (A.W.A.)
P.O. Box 321
Concord, N.H. 03301

U.S. Canoe Association
606 Ross Street
Middletown, Ohio 45042

LOCAL ORGANIZATIONS

Northeast

Appalachian Mountain Club
(several chapters along East Coast)

Sierra Club—Conn. Chapter
7 Tyler Rd.
Riverside, Conn. 06878

M.I.T. Whitewater Club
att. James Aiglin
R 6432 M.I.T.
Cambridge, Mass. 02139

Westfield River Whitewater Canoe Club
att. Merritt Andrews
90 West Silver St.
Westfield, Mass. 01085

Ledyard Canoe Club of Dartmouth
P.O. Box 9
Hanover, N.H. 03755

Sheldon Brook Canoe and Kayak Club
c/o Backcountry Outfitters
625 White Plains Rd.
Tarrytown, N.Y. 10591

Rhode Island Whitewater Club
att. Rist Bonnefond
10 Pond St.
Wakefield, R.I. 02879

Johnson Whitewater Club
Johnson State College
Box 649
Johnson, Vt. 05656

Middle Atlantic

Buck Ridge Ski Club
att. Mark Fawcett
R.D. #1 Box 426E
Hockessin, Del. 19707

Appalachian River Runners Federation
att. Joe Monohan
Box 107
McHenry, Md. 21541

Monoco Canoe Club
att. Henry Kelly
Box 244
Island Heights, N.J. 08732

Mohawk Canoe Club
att. Chris Nelson
11 Overlook Drive
Long Valley, N.J. 07853

Wanda Canoe Club
att. Mike Rubin
295 Linden Rd.
Wayne, N.J. 07470

Kayak and Canoe Club of N.Y.
att. Steve Armbruster
26 Ridgeway Ave.
West Orange, N.J. 07052

Wildwater Boating Club
att. George W. Mullen
Box 513
Boalsburg, Pa. 16827

Philadelphia Canoe Club
att. Dr. Paul Liebman
4900 Ridge Ave.
Philadelphia, Pa. 19128

Penn Hills Whitewater Canoe Club
att. James Catello
12200 Garland Ave.
Pittsburgh, Pa. 15235

Penn State Outing Club
Canoe Division
4 Intramural Building
University Park, Pa. 16802

Scudder Falls Wildwater Club
att. Dave Benham
795 River Rd.
Yardley, Pa. 17404

Canoe Cruisers Association
Box 572
Arlington, Va. 22216

Southeast

Watauga Whitewater Club
att. Richard Furman, M.D.
State Farm Rd.
Boone, N.C. 28607

Sierra Club—Canoe Section
att. Gordon Howard
P.O. Box 463
Clemson, S.C. 29631

Carolina Whitewater Canoeing Assoc.
att. Jerry Paul
3412 Harvard Ave.
Columbia, S.C. 29205

University of South Carolina Whitewater Club
P.O. Box 80090
Columbia, S.C. 29033

North Central

Belleville Whitewater Club
att. Linda Seaman
3 Oakwood
Belleville, Ill. 62223

Chicago Whitewater Assoc.
att. Pamela Allen
5460 S. Ridgewood Ct.
Chicago, Ill. 60629

University of Chicago Whitewater Club
att. Bruce Campbell
933 East 56th St.
Chicago, Ill. 60637

Whitewater Valley Canoe Club
att. Chuck Taylor
1032 Cliff St.
Brookville, Ind. 47012

Minnesota Canoe Assoc.
Box 14077
Minneapolis, Minn. 55414

Cascaders Canoe and Kayaks
att. Linda Jenson
4925 Emerson Ave. South
Minneapolis, Minn. 55409

South Central

Arkansas Canoe Club
att. Joel Freund
440 Mission St.
Fayetteville, Ark. 72701

Arnold Whitewater Assoc.
att. John J. Schuh
490 Pine Court
Arnold, Mo. 63010

Ozark Cruisers
att. Robert McKelvey
#1 Blue Acres Trailer Ct.
Columbia, Mo. 65201

Ozark Wilderness Waterways Club
P.O. Box 16032
Kansas City, Mo. 64112

Albuquerque Whitewater Club
att. Glenn Fowler
804 Warm Sands Drive S.E.
Albuquerque, N.M. 87112

Rio Grande River Runners
att. Buck Cully
2210 Central Ave. S.E.
Albuquerque, N.M. 87106

Texas Whitewater Assoc.
att. Thomas Cowden
P.O. Box 5264
Austin, Tex. 78763

Greater Fort Worth Sierra Club
P.O. Box 1057
Fort Worth, Tex. 76101

West

Asoen Kayak and Canoe Club
Box 1520
Aspen, Colo. 81611

Colorado Whitewater Assoc.
att. Deane Hall
4260 East Evans Ave.
Denver, Colo. 80222

C.S.U. Whitewater Club
att. James Stohlquist
Colorado State University
Fort Collins, Colo. 80523

Fib Ark Boat Races
att. John Carr
P.O. Box 762
Salida, Colo. 81201

Idaho Alpine Club

att. Whitewater Coordinator
P.O. Box 2885
Idaho Falls, Id. 83401

Sawtooth Wildwater Club
att. Roger Hazelwood
2355 Elm St.
Mountain Home, Id. 83647

Wasatch Whitewater Assoc.
att. Chris Spelius
161 South 11 East
Salt Lake City, Utah 84102

Northwest

Oregon Rafting Club
att. Joe Chappell
Rte. #1, Box 300
Hubbard, Ore. 97032

Wilderness Waterways
att. Bryce Whitmore
12260 Galice Rd.
Merlin, Ore. 97532

Oregon Canoe and Kayak Club
Box 692
Portland, Ore. 97205

Seattle Canoe Club
att. Dr. Thomas Blakely
1411 150th St. S.E.
Belleview, Wash. 98007

Washington Kayak Club
att. Dave Hamilton
17318 30th Ave. #M2
Seattle, Wash. 98118

California

Antioch Whitewater Club
att. Max Young
40 North Lake Drive
Antioch, Calif. 94509

Sierra Club—River Touring Section
att. Tom Allen
1943 Napa
Berkeley, Calif. 94546

Haystackers White Water Club
att. Tom Johnson
P.O. Box 675
Kernville, Calif. 93238

Feather River Kayak Club
att. Mike Schneller
1773 Broadway St.
Marysville, Calif. 95901

Sierra Club—Yokut Chapter
att. Sam Gardali
914 Stanford Ave.
Modesto, Calif. 95350

Sierra Club—Loma Prieta Paddlers
att. Kathy Blau
2710 Ramona St.
Palo Alto, Calif. 94306

Sierra Club—Bay Chapter
att. Joel DeYoung
1455 Union St. #10
San Francisco, Calif. 94109

San Joaquin YMCA Whitewater Club
att. Richard Humbley
640 North Center St.
Stockton, Calif. 95202

Bibliography

Local and Regional Guides

Adirondack Canoe Waters: North Flow. Paul Jamieson. Adirondack Mountain Club.

Appalachian Waters. Vol. 1, The Delaware River and its Tributaries. Vol. 2, The Hudson River and its Tributaries. Vol. 3, The Susquehanna River and its Tributaries. Vol. 4, Southeastern U.S. Rivers. Walter F. Burmeister. Boston: Appalachian Books, 1975.
> Thoroughly exhaustive treatment. Some unfortunate errors, but still a good reference book.

Blue Ridge Voyages, 4 vols. Roger Corbett and Louis J. Matacia. Matacia Pub., 1973.
> Good maps. Covers primarily Pennsylvania, Virginia, and West Virginia.

Canoeing Whitewater. Randy Carter. Boston: Appalachian Books, 1974.
> An excellent, thorough guide to Virginia, West Virginia, North Carolina, and parts of Tennessee.

Carolina Whitewater. Bob Benner. Available through ACA Book Service. Exploring the Little Rivers of New Jersey. James and Margaret Cawley. New Brunswick, N.J.: Rutgers University Press, 1974.
> New Jersey's most complete guide with fascinating historical notes. Little heavy white water. A classic.

Missouri Ozark Waterways. Oz Hawksley. Jefferson City, Mo.: Missouri Conservation Commission.
> Hawksley knows his rivers well. Factual mile-by-mile guide. The area's best.

River Runners' Guides to the Canyons of the Green and Colorado Rivers. The Powell Society. Vol. 1, Dinosaur National Monument and Vicinity. Vol. 2, Labyrinth, Stillwater, and Cataract Canyon. Vol. 3, Marble Gorge and Grand Canyon. Vol. 4, Desolation and Gray Canyons.
> A series of maps showing individual rapids. A good trip planner.

Oregon River Tours. John Garren. Touchstone Press, 1977.

Boating Trails for California Rivers. State of California Department of Navigation and Ocean Development.
> Actually the state's recreational rivers plan, but it happens to list and describe many of California's best whitewater streams.

Canoeing the Waters of California. Ann Dwyer. Available from ACA Book Service.

Guide to White Water in the Wisconsin Area. Andres Pukna. Hoofers Outing Club, Madison: University of Wisconsin.

New England Canoe Guide. Boston: Appalachian Mountain Club, 1976.
> About the best New England Guide. Great for planning trips.

New England Whitewater River Guide. Ray Gabler. Villanova, Pa.: Tobey Pub., 1975.
> A good format. Up to date.

No Horns Blowing: Canoeing Ten Great Rivers in Maine. Eben Thomas. Available from ACA Book Service.
> Good, solid information on where and how to run by an author who obviously loves it.

Virginia White Water. H. Roger Corbett. Seneca Press.
> Virginia's best. Answers all the paddler's questions about each river. Good maps.

Whitewater, Quietwater: A Guide to the Wild Rivers of Wisconsin, *Upper Michigan, and Northeast Minnesota.* Bob Palzer. Evergreen Paddleways, 1976.
> Factual and complete. This is the guide all the locals use. Individual rapids are described.

Wildwater West Virginia. Robert G. Burrell and Paul C. Davidson. McClain Pub., 1972.
> A good trip-planning guide.

Wildwater Touring. L. Scott Arighi. New York: Macmillan, 1974.
> Although actually a "how-to" book, it includes several area descriptions. Well done.

How-to Books

Basic River Canoeing. Robert E. McNair. American Camping, 1969.
> A little old, but full of solid open-boat handling information.

Boat Builders Manual. Charles Walbridge. Available through ACA Book Service.
> Good wildwater designs.

Canoeing. American Red Cross.
> Excellent guide to paddling technique and water reading. Best for open boaters.

The Complete Wilderness Paddler. James West Davidson and John Rugge. New York: Alfred Knopf, 1976.
> Very readable and informative. Two men take a long wilderness open-canoe trip. You learn much from their experience.

Kayaking: The New Whitewater Sport for Everyone. Robert R. Anderson and Jay Evans. Greene Pub. Available through ACA Book Service.
> One of the few good kayak instruction books. Some topics are excluded, but what is covered is covered well.

Pole, Paddle, Portage. Bill Riviere. New York: Van Nostrand Reinhold, 1974.
> A smattering of everything, from portage techniques to equipment selection. Better for polers than paddlers.

White Water Handbook for Canoe and Kayak. John T. Urban, ed. Appalachian Mountain Club, 1972.
> A little outdated, but still thorough and readable. Good for open or decked canoes.

Classics

Canoeing with the Cree. Eric Sevareid. Minnesota Historical Society, 1968. (Reprint of 1935 edition.)
> At 17 the news analyst paddled alone from Minnesota to Hudson Bay. A fascinating story.

The Exploration of the Colorado River and its Canyons. John Wesley Powell. Dover, 1895.
> A real classic. The one-armed major's exploration of the Grand Canyon is one of the greatest true adventure stories.

On the River. Walter Magnes Teller. New Brunswick, N.J.: Rutgers University Press, 1976.
> Selections from journals of Thoreau, Chichester, and eleven other early river explorers. Fascinating.

Rushton and his Times in American Canoeing. Atwood Manley. Syracuse: Syracuse University Press, 1968.
> This famous boatbuilder and explorer gives the full flavor of the Adirondacks in the 19th century.

Survival of the Bark Canoe. John McPhee. New York: Farrar Straus and Giroux, 1975.
> Story of a man who learned the primitive art of building bark canoes and dedicated himself to keeping it alive.

To the Arctic by Canoe. C. Stuart Houston, ed. Montreal: McGill-Queens University Press, 1974.
> Robert Hood's original journal and magnificent paintings of the English-Canadian Arctic Expedition, 1819-1821.

Index

Acknowledgments

ACKNOWLEDGMENTS

In researching this book I have had the help of a great number of associates who gave freely of their time and experience. It is impossible to acknowledge them all, but I would like to give special thanks to Tom Aluni, Al Button, Tom Daniels, Dave Barnhardt, Larry Jamieson, Robert Woodward, Tom Johnson, Dr. John T. Baker, Scott Arighi, Cully Erdman, Fred Young, Dave Gale, Warren Yeisley, and Tom Jackson.